Mix, Mend, Mold:

Owning My Story & Finding My Freedom

By Dayna Altman

Dedication

This book is dedicated to those who smile even when they are sad. May you find comfort in this authentic account of a girl who decided to take off "the smiling mask." You are just as worthy a human when you are sad just as you are happy.

Thank You

Ingredients:

-Shannon Luders-Manuel -Editor
-Jason SonDu Taglieri - Graphic Designer
-Brenna Stewart - Photographer
-Dena B. Tranen - Epilogue

Preface

I have been writing a version of this memoir since I was thirteen years old. From as early as I can remember, writing has been a go-to outlet: so many moments feeling as though my world was ending, and so much solace found in pen to paper, or fingers to keyboard.

So here I am fourteen years later at twenty-seven years old, making it happen. I had previously thought I would wait until I was "older and wiser" to write my memoir. I mean, who writes a memoir before thirty anymore?

Come to find out actually it's not that unheard of, and, for me, I would like to do something to commemorate the work I have done in this first chapter of my life. If I have learned anything about myself in this life it's that I will never have it "all figured out"—but I'm not sure any of us do. We are all constantly evolving, so why not capture what I have learned so far?

I was inspired to begin writing this in the midst of the COVID-19 crisis. When I first found out that I may be subject to self-quarantine and social distancing with the rest of the country, I was scared. There have been some "normal" weekends in the past that have felt so scary in the confines of my own brain that a mandated "isolation" felt terrifying, and yet, here I am writing. I am writing to make sense of the things that I can't. I am writing to recognize how far I have come, and I am writing in hopes of inspiring readers to be okay with not having it all figured out yet... and doing something big anyway. Leaning into our own stories and giving people the space to find their voice is my passion, and it has been one of the greatest gifts I feel I have given to myself and to the world around me.

This all really started in the summer of 2017. I had just survived a serious car accident, and it was a summer with naturally little structure. Not having a car in suburban Southboro, Massachusetts, only complicated my situation, as the transportation limitations left me walking six-tenths of a mile to the local Dunkin' every morning and lying in my bed after the excursion every afternoon. Contrastly, a month before, I had "wrapped" my first documentary, entitled *Life After: The Film,* and that changed my life in so many ways. You see, I have been creating projects, initiatives and organizations to change and better the world since I was in elementary school. However, creating something as tangible as a documentary film helped me take my work more seriously. Itching to bring something else into the world—while stuck at my parents' house in the height of summer with no car—left me with little options.

I have never been someone who felt confident in the kitchen. Growing up, I never cooked or baked, and dinner in my family looked like nightly Lean Cuisines with baked smiley fries. I was surprised when I found some peace in the kitchen through baking that summer. I quickly learned that baking is precise, while cooking is creative. And while I identify as a creative entrepreneurial artist, there is something to be said for some structure and precision. With my world out of control in so many ways, measuring a ¼ cup of flour helped make things feel a little more in control.

As the summer came to an end, I eventually got a new car, and I returned to campus for grad school classes. When the weather turned colder and some normalcy fell into place, my baking became more sporadic. I re-entered the smallest apartment I imagine I will ever live in, and my time quickly became consumed by homework. But a fire stayed ignited inside of me. It wasn't about and never will be about the baking. But it's about the connection, the community and the comfort people have found within the context of food. The way we share with each other, the way we learn from each other when it comes to a recipe or a meal. It began to be about pairing something difficult to discuss (mental health) with something normal, and watching conversation develop—and something clicked. As a mental health advocate and activist for so many years, I recognized the need for connection and community in the mental health world. So I combined the two (mental health and baking), and I have never looked back.

In all honesty, I have had to become a much better baker since the publication of my mental health and resilience cookbook in July 2019. *Bake it Till You Make it: Breaking Bread, Building Resilience* was my first introduction to the concept of pairing recipes, resource pages and storytelling, bound together and sold on Amazon and at Target. It changed my life and continues to do so. I have helped others find their voices, and I have come to explore new ways to tell my own story and find the confidence to do so through various presentations, my favorite being *Bake it Till You Make it: Live!* This is a presentation in which I put on a cooking demonstration and draw metaphors between the ingredients, the cooking methods and my own story. This is a really special combination and is how I have chosen to structure this book, in honor of the brand and legacy that I have created.

Cake pops were the first recipe I embarked on in the original mental health cookbook and the recipe in which I have chosen to use while sharing my story here. There are so many steps to the recipe, and yet each one allows for unique decoration, a combination of flavors and methodical practice. There is room for creativity, for mistakes and for conversation. The best part of the cake pop-making process is that you have to take the cake apart in order to shape it and put it back together again.

So here I am, taking apart my life in hopes of better understanding it and to provide some comfort, inspiration or light to those who may be going through something they feel will only break them. While I don't have all the answers and I am still trying very much to figure it all out, I hope you find comfort in my story to keep going, because like in the world of cake pops, coming apart is just the beginning.

PREHEAT THE OVEN TO 350F

Like food needs an oven to bake, my "oven" or environment in many ways shaped me as a child and as a person. The house I have always called home is blue. It has a two-car garage, a swing set in the back and a finished basement. There is a basketball hoop in the driveway, and the lawn is nicely manicured (sometimes). It sits only a few miles away from a well-respected public school system, a library and a convenience store.

BEGIN BY PREHEATING THE OVEN: 150F

Growing up in the affluent town of Southboro, Massachusetts, I didn't know much outside of my community. I always thought I was "poor" because I lived on the "south side" of town. I thought that if I didn't have a house with a pool or my own bathroom that I was the odd one out. I have come to realize these thoughts bring with them unfathomable privilege.

Living in Southboro also brought endless opportunities. Everyone went on a cruise over February break, and all of the eighth graders got to go to Washington D.C., as a class trip. All of my peers in elementary school had been to Disney World at least once, and I was no different. I looked around and saw support. I had some really nice teachers; my kindergarten teacher even said she wanted to be my friend. I also had really supportive parents, so I didn't know why I felt so unhappy.

—-

I don't remember much from the first family meeting, other than sitting on the floor of my living room. My dad had tears in his eyes when he told my sister and me that he and my mom would be separating. My mind went blank at that moment; I couldn't really process it or put any words to how I was feeling. Instead I asked if "we would still go to Disney World." And it has taken me years of therapy to relinquish the shame I carried over my younger self asking that question in that moment.

My dad moved to an apartment building that my sister and I called "the place." I can remember getting new comforters and decorations for my new room, but I never felt settled. As a scared eight-year-old, I just wanted my parents back together and could care less about the new material items.

One Saturday morning at "the place," I woke up with a pimple on my face. I was surprised to see something so red and shiny on my skin. I went to my dad asking him what to do; he hesitated, saying this was something my mom could handle, and I broke down in silence. I couldn't cry outwardly, so my turmoil became internal. I didn't want to wait until I saw my mom during the week, and I certainly just wanted things back to the way they were. As clearly as I can articulate those feelings in this moment, when I generally think back to that time, I always picture myself in the same way: smiling and silent. Smiling to be pleasing, "totally fine" to protect my younger sister (the absolute best I could), and silent to make sure everyone else was okay, when I was dying inside.

During the week, my sister and I were with my mom. I again have few, sporadic memories of the period of time we lived with her without my dad. Even before my parents' separation, my mom struggled with food and her body. From the minute I could under-stand the words "I hate," I knew almost intuitively that the next words were going to be "my body." Every week was a new diet: cabbage soup, Jenny Craig, South Beach, Weight Watchers. When my dad wasn't around, my mom took my sister and me to Weight Watchers meetings, since she could never miss a meet-ing. The messages I heard at Weight Watchers continue to live within the context of my own eating disorder. "Don't be the garbage can," they would say. I knew my mom hated her body and had a terrible relationship with food, but this was solidified when I heard her purge for the first time. It was around this time that vomit became the thing I feared the most in the world. The idea of being sick, feeling sick, seeing vomit... I could barely utter the word. And yet it was happening, all the time, and my mom was making herself do it.

A few months later, I woke up one morning and my dad came home. It was like God answered my prayers. But my fears and worries didn't stop. I continued to fear vomit, and I began to worry about school excessively. I repeated my spelling words over and over and over again to prepare for spelling tests. I began to take longer looks at myself in the mirror and compare myself to other girls in my class: analyzing bodies and constantly seeking reassurance from my mom that I was pretty, thin and that she (my mom) didn't hate me. The fear of being hated and asking my parents and sister if they were mad at me became compulsive, as did my need to say sorry. At one point I remember not even recognizing why or what I was saying.

With an overwhelming culmination of emotions, I sought theater as an outlet—at first because it was time I got alone with my mom. It was something we both liked, and I genuinely loved being on stage. Whether it was the energy of my astrological sign (Leo), or being a natural extrovert, or both, there was something about being in the spotlight that I loved. Maybe it was because all I wanted was to be seen, even if it meant being acknowledged as a character or as someone else.

2004: A family vacation in Los Angeles, California. We had a tour of Beverly Hills in a Red Mustang Convertible. We thought we were real celebrities.

This was a trip during Summer vacation 2008. We went to Puerto Rico as a family. I was scared of this slide, I am happy my sister went with me.

My family spent the end of every summer in Wildwood, New Jersey from the time I was three until
the summer I turned nineteen. This was my sister
and me on the beach in 1998.

Sitting on the same steps I walked down from the time I could walk-to present. This is one of my all time favorite photos with my dad from 1993.

I would still match with my sister to this day if she would let me. Usually when she sees me wearing a similar outfit in our adulthood, she changes. I don't blame her but I will always treasure the days we could wear the same hat without her taking it off. My sister, Jamie and I in our house in Southboro in 2004.

A photo on stage performing in *Joseph & The Amazing Technicolor Dreamcoat* in 2005. I sang "One More Angel in Heaven" as the brother, Simon, in this show. I got to perform alongside some of my best theater friends and my sister, Jamie (in the right corner).

A backstage photo from *Seussical* in 2010 with friends: Kate, Avery and Dan. Rest in peace always, Dan, we miss you.

My mom and I backstage during *Seussical: The Musical.* This was one of my biggest roles ever, not to mention a dream role! I played Gertrude McFuzz and my mom played Mrs. Mayor in this production.

I am so lucky to have spent six summers at the ultimate theater camp: Stagedoor Manor! My best friend from camp, Molly and I on our way to the movies.

My first and last performance pretending I was a Rocket in 2009. Lucky to have made this forever friend, Julie, during the Christmas Spectacular.

OVEN PREHEAT: 200F

Like most theater kids, shows came with an introduction to several passions in the arts. I started taking voice lessons and acting classes and began to really take my dance classes seriously. When my friends came over to "play," I directed and starred in shows we created in my basement. Most of them had music, some had important themes and I even started my own traveling theater company in fifth grade: "The Not So Off Broadway Players." We performed often at community events and assisted living centers.

When I entered middle school, my theater career really took off, and I was doing three shows at once as well as obsessing, stressing and crying over school. In sixth grade we read *Tuck Everlasting*—my first book that I had to read at the breakfast table because rehearsal ran so late. But, did I want to give up the place where I found love, attention and comfort? To compensate, I just got better at putting myself in overdrive, picking up small rituals here and there to ensure things would not flow out of control. For example, before I went to bed, I checked that the sink drained and that the toilet flushed about ten times. I spinned in circles looking in the sink, then the toilet, then back, until I could look at myself in the mirror and go to bed.

This worked for a while, until my sister and I learned my parents would be separating again. This time it was more unclear. No identified "place," and no timeframe. My sister and I sat in her room, coloring pictures for each other, in case we would be separated like Hallie and Annie in *The Parent Trap*. Much to our relief, this separation did not last long, but my mom leaving the dinner table to cry started to become a pattern. I would follow my mom upstairs to check on her, which started to create a divide in the family. My mom and I became close, and my sister and my dad paired off.

If my mom didn't run upstairs, she left in her car. Those were the worst nights because I had no idea if she would ever come back.

She reassured me every night that if she ran away she would take me with her; that never really felt settling to me, even though I truly believe she thought she was saying the right thing. This set the tone for our relationship. We would ask each other for reassurance, negate the positive, and go back to hating our bodies and ourselves. We started exploring diets together and made a pact that we wouldn't get our stomachs stapled because apparently, you could die from it.

My mom truly became the only person who understood me, and I think she felt the same.

OVEN PREHEAT: 250F

In eighth grade, things changed. I was part of a large group of friends in middle school. We all loved theater and auditioned for the same shows. I felt voiceless in the group at times and never felt special. Our lunch conversations were either about calories, other girls or musical theater. These girls became meaner and more vicious over the years—including creating a petition that stated one of the girls was to leave the lunch table and the friend group.

As much as I wanted to fit in, and though I shopped at the same stores as my friends, there was a part of me that wanted my own time to shine. So, I went to audition for a show on my own. This truly rocked the foundation of the friend group. I was called a sneaky snake. I was asked not to sit with the group, and, worst of all, I moved to the bottom of or totally off my "friends'" BFF lists on their AIM profiles. In 2005, AIM or AOL Instant Messenger was one of the only social media platforms for tweens, and, to me, it impacted the way I saw myself. While the name implied the purpose was to be instant messaging with friends, in my world it was not about the communication; it was about the profile. It took hours to build an AIM profile. The top part of my friends' profiles usually had quotes from the movie *Rent,* typed in hot pink font, but the most important part was the friends list on the bottom. Girls in the group listed their friends in order of how much they liked them. Seeing my initials last or erased totally from profiles destroyed my self-worth. If I didn't have friends, what did I have?

And it wasn't like I could really find new ones. I could map out the cafeteria of my middle school. There was no room for me to "switch groups"; if the girls in that group excluded me from their lunch table and their profiles, it meant I was completely alone.

Every day for months, I came home crying after school. I ran upstairs to my bedroom, got to the door and slammed it. My mom and sister then sat on the other side of the door, begging me to come out, passing notes back and forth, pleading with me to leave my room. At the time, I thought hiding was what I was supposed to do. I felt alone in every capacity, and I felt so much shame—damaged as a person and unlovable as a friend and daughter. I proclaimed to my parents that I was a "mistake," not truly understanding what it meant to say this, but feeling I wasn't meant to be on this earth. And this was the first time I contemplated suicide.

One day after dance class, I sat on the floor of my bedroom with my mom, hysterically crying, begging her not to make me go to school, and telling her I would do anything to not go, even if that meant I was dead. This scared my parents, but they didn't know what to do. They had no idea there were resources in the community and figured once I started at a regional high school, I would feel "better." They thought I would surround myself with a new group of friends from the neighboring town. And in some ways, it did get better. I had a new group of friends in high school, but I never quite felt like I fit in. I tried to find ways to connect with them. I always knew I wanted to "change the world" in some way, so I created projects that they supported. Whether it was the "Pink Out for Breast Cancer" I created as the president of the National Honors Society or the fundraising I did at a local fair, I did my best to invite my friends into my world. This didn't stop me, though, from using my grades as an external measure to validate and rate my worth. Outside of my mission to change the world; outside of my hobbies that included voice lessons, theater and dance; school came before everything. I wanted an external measure (my grades) to tell me I was "good enough." So, I worked as hard as I could in school. I sharpened ten pencils every night before going to school the next day, aligning each on my desk with the best eraser choices closest to me. It was odd, but no one said anything—other than a terrible history teacher who thought it was funny to hip check my desk so they all fell to the ground.

During my junior year of high school, each time I came downstairs for breakfast with swollen eyes from crying, my parents asked me if I wanted to see a therapist. Every time, I said, "No... no..." because I was embarrassed and I was scared. The look of relief I saw on my dad's face only made it harder to continue to say "no... no." I knew they didn't want to believe I needed to see a therapist. Not because of stigma—though I am sure the wine moms of Northboro/Southboro would have found it fun to talk about—but because they didn't want to believe I felt as bad as I did. Why would they? They gave me so much. A beautiful home, food to eat, the most fashionable clothes, access to all extracurricular activities, vacations at least three times a year and love (although it was hard for me to let it in).

Outside of grades, weight was my validator. I hid this inside for the most part, except one day it came out at the ballet barre. During dance class, one of my peers said she was struggling to put on weight, and I said, "I wish I had that problem." My dance teacher was alarmed and told me she wanted to speak to my mom after class. I ran to my mom's car and apologized before my teacher could even get to her. My mom looked confused as to why this was concerning. She said she would have said the exact same thing.

OVEN PREHEAT 300F

My safe food list became smaller and my grades felt more important, as each year of high school passed. When it was time to look at colleges, I already knew Boston University (BU) was my first choice. My favorite teacher had gone there, it had a great secondary education program and it was in the city. I applied early decision in hopes of becoming a middle school English teacher, because I knew how hard middle school could be. I got deferred during the early decision process, which meant my application would be re-evaluated with regular decision applicants. My high school guidance counselor told me that I was a great candidate aside from my SAT scores, which crushed me in the application process. I never have been and never will be a "good" test taker, and unfortunately that limited my college process. I applied to nine other schools, and when I got rejected from BU officially in April 2010, Providence College fell into my lap as the only school that really made "sense" otherwise.

I found out I got rejected from BU after my first spring performance in my high school's production of *Guys and Dolls*. The night before I checked the portal, I stayed up all night believing if I thought about it enough I would get in. I went to my family computer and read "We regret to inform you..." I left the computer and walked over to the kitchen counter and started ripping up the Providence College welcome packet. I never let myself get angry, but in that moment, I was devastated. When I was done tearing apart the packet, I decided to put it back together and start reading it. I started to imagine myself in the environment, and it became ok.

OVEN PREHEAT SET: 350F

The summer before college, I was a mess and hanging on by a thread. I tried my best to move on "business as usual." I spent my seventh and last summer at Stagedoor Manor performing arts training center (aka the ultimate theater camp), and I went to my college orientation. I was packing amidst "green couch therapy," in which I would sit on the green couch in my living room and make a list of everything that was "wrong." But once again no one knew. This internal pain, struggle and mess was totally contained within the walls of my house and even more so within the confines of my mind. On the outside, I was the happiest girl around: I always smiled and I always looked put together, so why would anyone think differently? Right before I went to college, my family and I went to New York City for our annual Broadway show trip. It was on this trip that I had my first classified panic attack.

It was over ninety degrees that day, and the air was so sticky it was hard to breathe. I felt so anxious that I became nauseous. This had happened a few times before at restaurants earlier in the summer. I would get so overwhelmed that I needed to go outside for air. This time the nausea was overwhelming, and because I was outside already, there was nothing to do but panic. I was hyperventilating on 41st Street when my mom told me therapy was free in college and that it would really help me. It was the only thing about college that I was really excited for, but I knew college itself wasn't optional. I think two students in my high school class of 354 did not plan to attend a four-year college or university after high school graduation, and I never dreamt of doing anything else. But the idea of being in a new environment, away from my parents, scared me, maybe even more than vomit.

I turned 16 surrounded by my best friends in high school. I celebrated at the Melting Pot with eight of my friends and remember how much I loved this Jessica McClintok dress.

September 2009: My seventeenth birthday was celebrated with the ultimate Murder Mystery birthday party in my back-yard. Here I am with one of my best friends, Alyssa! My mom has always made my birthday a big deal, probably why I still treasure every August 20th.

One of my last days of High School, with one of my closest friends, Gillian! May 2010.

June 2010: My sister, Jamie and I at my High School graduation.

Algonquin Regional High School graduation with one of my
oldest and closest friends, Fiona.

✓ PREHEAT THE OVEN TO 350F

BAKER'S NOTES

BEGIN TO MAKE CAKE BY FOLLOWING THE INSTRUCTIONS ON THE CAKE MIX BOX.

ADD THE FOLLOWING INGREDIENTS:

1 CUP OF WATER

To this day, I can't chew spearmint gum without thinking of the day I moved into the McVinney freshman residence Hall at Providence College (PC) in August 2010. Even though I packed every stuffed animal I had and my favorite outfits from Forever 21, mint gum was the only thing that really brought me comfort during this change because it curbed my anxious stomach. I moved into the dorm earlier than most of my friends from high school. I would be starting an early program at PC called "Urban Action (UA)." This consisted of several days of community service in the Providence area while simultaneously becoming accustomed to the school and the environment. I met some of my best friends during UA and actually thought I may be able to do the college thing. I found this time foundational, like water can be for anything that needs to grow.

—-

⅓ CUP OF OIL

While water is a growing property for cake, oil makes it tender (both in the cases of cake pops and all other baked goods), and the moment classes started, I found myself in my most tender state. On the first day of classes, I had a panic attack. When I took my seat, I heard nothing but the sound of my unrhythmic breathing. Sweat began to drop from my forehead and I had the overwhelming feeling that I needed to leave. So, I did. This is how I functioned in school for the first few weeks, until it dawned on me that I was missing more classes than I was attending, and if I didn't measure my worth through my grades, what did I have? How was I going to get good grades if I missed class? How would I be a good person if I didn't have good grades?

This all hit me in the early afternoon on a Tuesday in late September. There was a big tree on lower campus that I would cry under while my friends brought me Sprite and Saltines. I continuously felt a lump in my throat and that I was going to get sick every day. My friends brought me from my tree to the counseling center. They saw I needed help, and I didn't know what to do to access it, so they brought me to find it. The wait to see a therapist was about two weeks unless it was an emergency. I hesitated but put a smile on my face and pleasantly let the woman at the front desk know it was not an emergency. For the record, not functioning is an emergency, but I wanted to be pleasing, I wanted to be lovely and in no way did I want to disturb anyone's schedule, so I waited.

On campus, I was able to see a psychiatrist, a mental health doctor that can prescribe medication, before I eventually saw my first therapist about a week later. My psychiatrist immediately prescribed me medicine and diagnosed me with generalized anxiety, depression and an eating disorder.

CRACK THREE EGGS

CRACK EGG ONE: Anxiety

When I found out I was diagnosed with a generalized anxiety disorder, I took an incredible sigh of relief. Finally! There was a word for what I was feeling, and it put into perspective so many moments up to this point. I started two different medications and was hoping they would help the anxiety evaporate. Weeks passed and things felt less acute, but by no means did I feel "cured." I still felt like I was breaking. I was able to reinvest in my life though at times. I started going to class and was able to sit through it. I applied for every student group on campus, and while I got rejected from pretty much all of them, I kept trying. I even met my first boyfriend of two months. I was able to put the smile back on my face in a place of high-functioning anxiety.

I saw my first therapist at Providence College in October. I don't remember much about him other than he had a small sandbox on the arm of the patient chair. Every time I went to see him, I moved the sand in the box back and forth. I had a hard time opening up to him, and it just became harder each week. This was the first time I had ever gone to therapy, and I had no idea what to expect or that you could even ask for a different therapist if you felt uncomfortable. With the end of the fall semester, I asked my psychiatrist if I could start seeing a female therapist. She set it up for me for when I came back to PC in the spring.

CRACK EGG TWO: Depression

The first therapy appointment I ever had with Dr. M felt more comfortable and natural than my whole fall with the man. She was easy to talk to, and we did some exploring. I seemed to find a way to cope with my anxiety, but it left me feeling empty. In some ways the sadness became overwhelming, and each day I was breaking down more and more. I felt very alone even in the dining hall with fifteen friends sitting beside me who loved me. I began to think back to the way I felt in high school. So many years and situations that my parents and I had labeled the "teenage blues" I was now realizing it was probably more extreme. I cried in therapy pretty much every session, but when I left, I never looked happier. This was one of my biggest barriers to finding treatment and being taken seriously. Even in therapy I wanted to be "liked" or "loved," and I was convinced that was only doable with a smile and "being adorable." Being adorable felt like being loved. It felt like from the outside, maybe if I was lovable and maybe if I was cute enough, then I would be ok.

As the months passed, seeking therapy was something my dad really supported, but my mom did not as much. I think she was worried that she would come up. As she told me "all therapists place some type of blame on the mother." This made it hard at first to talk to Dr. M about my family. I didn't want to upset my mom, nor did I want to believe there was anything wrong with her or my family structure. Burying this at first felt hard, until I recognized I could make it all go away.

CRACK EGG THREE: Restriction, Diagnosed EDNOS

When I recognized that restricting my food could make everything stop, it was the only thing that mattered. I was good at it. I had been restricting food and making lists of my calories since learning about "the trash can" at Weight Watchers in elementary school. I tried the cabbage soup diet, learning the guidelines from my mom. I was even restricting my food intake throughout my entire senior year of high school, but no one ever noticed.

At PC, people noticed. I was so anxious all the time that restricting felt effortless. I constantly had a lump in my throat and in my head that felt like I was going to vomit, so not eating felt like the safest option. I would go to the dining hall with my friends and push food around on my plate—usually something from the salad bar and half a peanut butter and jelly sandwich. I remember my well-meaning friends telling me that it was scary to see me like this. That putting coffee in my body with no food was dangerous, that I should eat two peanut butter and jelly sandwiches. But I found a way to cope. Not only did I cope, I found a way to be loved.

People supported the way I looked, and I felt the outpour of love I think I was searching for, for a long time. I wish we lived in a society in which someone's drastic weight loss was met with concern and compassion rather than "Tell me everything!!" But that is not the world we live in (yet anyway).

Restricting kept my depression at bay. I didn't have much room in my mind to think about anything but what I would not be eating for the next meal, which protected me from thinking about anything the least bit depressing. I was also convinced that I had figured out how to manage my anxiety. Little food-in made it a low risk that I would get sick, and on the surface this is what my anxiety revolved around. I kept going to therapy and I continued to take my medication, but I was not completely "there." My crack was internal, and I don't think there were moments I even recognized it.

Dr. M diagnosed me with EDNOS, which is Eating Disorder Not Otherwise Specified. I was restricting but I did not meet the low weight requirement for a full diagnosis of anorexia. Reading this on my paperwork crushed me. I felt like I could not even "do an eating disorder right." My self-hatred and self-disgust grew daily, even if the support and attention I got for my weight loss put me in the light.

✓ PREHEAT THE OVEN TO 350F

✓ BEGIN TO MAKE CAKE BY ADDING:
  1 CUP WATER
  1/3 CUP OIL
  3 EGGS

BAKER'S NOTES

(PANIC! •.... ANXIETY ..... DEPRESSION ~z²THE □ not enough EDNOS ~SONGS)

What I brought to PC (INTERNAL)

what I brought to PC... (OUTSIDE)

BOWS/HEADBANDS   CLOTHES   /SHOES   BEDDING I BATH

MIX INGREDIENTS IN A BOWL

Come spring semester of my freshman year, I was in a routine. I weighed myself in the morning, went to class, saw friends, weighed myself again, did homework, weighed myself, went to bed.

In February, I found out some of my friends were joining PC Dance Club. It turned out that there were several options to get involved. I signed up for two "numbers": one jazz and one ballet. The ballet number was set to "Bohemian Rhapsody" by Queen. The first few days of rehearsals for "Bohemian Rhapsody" were difficult, but I found I loved the freedom to dance again. The choreographer was a senior, Lilly, and one day I talked to her after class. She took me under her wing in that exact moment, and I will forever be grateful for that. Lilly saw my behavior and she listened to me every day. Lunch with Lilly became less about dance, and more about sisterhood. She told me she recognized everything I was going through because she had gone through the exact same thing. She suggested I look into eating disorder treatment, which I called "rehab" for the first few months of even having the idea in my head. "Rehab" meant I would receive more "intense" and consistent treatment rather than going to "outpatient" therapy appointments once a week.

Lilly sought treatment at the Klarman Program at a place called McLean Hospital. I remember I went to her house and we sat on her porch so I could call Klarman and ask for an intake. It didn't work like that and there was a waitlist, so I went to Dr. M instead. She was very proud of me for asking for help. And while this is unusual—as most of the time when someone seeks mental health treatment, it is an emergency and there is little investigating done by the patient—this was different. I was not in such a compromised position this was immediate; rather, I started to tour different treatment facilities for the summer with my parents. I remember when my dad came to pick me up from PC to take me on a tour of one facility, he was scared to see me at first, but he didn't realize that while my body had changed, nothing in my mind had. I was struggling with these thoughts and this disorder for so long. I wish my world could have seen it when it wasn't so obvious, but it was hard for me to tell anyone how much I was struggling when it was generally normalized behavior for the Altman women. I remember one facility I visited felt supportive. It was a welcoming environment and it was residential.

Residential treatment meant that I would be in the program for a few weeks, living in the facility, able to get help in the evenings and on the weekends. This felt important to me. I knew where my mom was with her eating disorder, and I did not think I could go to a partial (or day) program and come home to feel negated or feel I had freedom to "cheat." Everything would feel jumbled and mixed if I lived in one reality during the day and another at my parents' house. However, my insurance denied my acceptance into the residential program. Again, I didn't meet the weight minimum, which led to so many feelings of shame and guilt. I wrapped my head around going to a day program, and I started on a Thursday in late May.

✓ PREHEAT THE OVEN TO 350F

✓ BEGIN TO MAKE CAKE BY ADDING:
  1 CUP WATER
  1/3 CUP OIL
  3 EGGS

✓ MIX INGREDIENTS IN A BOWL

BAKER'S NOTES

I am lucky to have made such close and true friends at PC, like Caro, pictured here. As painful as this time was, I do remember enjoying this weekend when my sister (middle) came to visit.

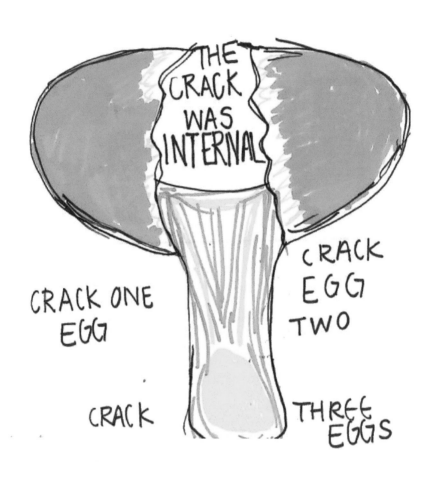

BAKE FOR 18-20 MINUTES

I walked into the small "partial program", day room on Hope Avenue feeling like this was the first day of the rest of my life. A mix of my life's circumstances and "ingredients," up until this point, I felt an unrelenting need for help. Immediately entering the program, I was introduced to the other patients and my treatment team, which consisted of a case manager and nutritionist. The case manager was an acting therapist while I was in the program: setting up family meetings, organizing a treatment plan and providing individual support. The nutritionist was helping me design a meal plan and stick to weight related goals. I was nervous entering this new territory, but I knew I wanted to learn and I wanted help. I quickly began to see that getting help was going to be a lot harder than I thought. First, I didn't really click with my case manager in the program. I found her very invalidating and hard to talk to. I did find a counselor, Laura, who ran groups during the day and had meals with us, whom I trusted. Laura was considered to be a day counselor or "floor staff" and not part of my treatment team per say, but I trusted Laura. She and I sat outside during break times and threw a stress ball back and forth. I told her I didn't really feel understood in the program and that my anxiety was just getting worse. I also started to feel increasingly depressed. My logic was, I was trying to better myself, so why was I not getting better? Why didn't showing up mean that I would just become okay again?

These feelings only continued to bake and bubble at home. My parents were confused by the process as much as I was. They both thought the food on my meal plan was "way too much," and there was little support at home to keep up with that plan on the weekend. I felt every day that I was choosing my recovery or my family, and I wanted my family more than anything.

Things were only complicated by my mom. Like before, we connected through our eating disorders, but now I was working toward recovery and she had no interest in that. Instead, my mom would help me pack my lunch before treatment and had suggestions on how to "cheat" the system. For example, my mom encouraged me to take the "low calorie" label off Babybel Light Cheese. Babybel cheese has a plastic wrapper on the outside of its red wax packaging. My mom thought that taking the plastic piece off and bringing the cheese in its unlabeled red wax would be a good way to sneak something "low calorie" into the day program. She didn't think anyone would think anything of an un-labeled piece of cheese. I didn't want to cheat. I never broke any rules because I always wanted to be a "good girl," but I wanted love from my mom more, so I held my breath when Laura went through my lunch the next day. She didn't notice, but I hated my-self for this. I continuously told myself I couldn't have it both ways and yelled at myself in my head until I burst into tears.

"What is wrong with you?" I'd ask myself. "Do you want to get better or not?"

My depression became louder, and my peers in treatment had the answers: self-harm. It wasn't abnormal for my peers to seek other ways to hurt themselves, and on a night that was especially hard, I decided I to try it. I didn't feel a rush or a relief, or really anything but worse. I didn't know how to express how bad I felt if it wasn't visible by my low body weight. This seemed like a good alterna-tive even though it was accompanied with more self-hatred.

Towards the end of my five weeks in the eating disorder treatment partial program, I searched for a therapist. My therapist at PC was not seeing clients in the summer, and I wasn't prepared to drive back and forth each week to see a different one there. I tried two therapists before I found "the one." My mom liked the first one since she was a retired actress; I couldn't stand the second one, but the third one was cool, and her name is Kathy.

✓ PREHEAT THE OVEN TO 350F

✓ BEGIN TO MAKE CAKE BY ADDING:
  1 CUP WATER
  1/3 CUP OIL
  3 EGGS

✓ MIX INGREDIENTS IN A BOWL

✓ BAKE FOR 18-20 MINUTES

BAKER'S NOTES

Walking into my first day of treatment felt like the first day of the rest of my life.

Although Baybel cheese is delicious, it definitely holds a lot of painful memories with it. This is my take on drawing the label.

The Boston Bruins won the Stanley Cup in 2011. My dad and I went to the parade on a weekend while I was in treatment in June. It was nice to connect with him in this way even amongst what I was going through.

LET CAKE COOL

Kathy came as a therapist recommendation from a family friend. She ran her practice out of her house and always had me put my feet up. She brought me a diet coke with ice for every session and sat with me in my pain. She listened to me in a way that I don't think any other therapist had, or maybe didn't know how to. I felt safe with Kathy in a way that I did not feel safe anywhere else in the world or in my body. She reassured me there was no comparison of misery, that everything I was feeling was valid, and that "honey, you are just going to be ok." Even though Kathy was my safe "place," I still struggled every moment I was not in therapy.

Crying, restricting, burning myself, I was desperate for a change. My family tried supporting me and comforting me, and my dad even offered me a simple job at his office for structure. I had no idea what I needed. Suicide was something that I was considering more and more. I had suicidal ideations, even during my time in the eating disorder-focused partial program, and yet, it just seemed to get worse. It was all-consuming and all I could think about. I remember the day I told Kathy I could not guarantee that I would not continue to think about a plan and method. So, she took action, and the next day my mom was driving me to East House at McLean Hospital.

McLean Hospital, a prestigious institution where both the movies *Girl Interrupted* and *Running from Crazy* have significant cameos, is one of the most respected mental health facilities in the world. I don't think I knew that when I walked in the doors of 2East (East House) on July 27, 2011. All I knew was I was scared. I was relieved once again to be getting help but also worried that it was going to be like the partial program. But I wanted it to be different. So, before dinner on my first night, I walked right up to one of the floor staff and told her, "I have an eating disorder, so meals here might be hard for me."

This moment started a more honest stay at 2East, and right away I settled into treatment. I had a roommate doing a parallel program on the same floor. 2East is a program for adolescents/teens who are struggling with anxiety, depression and suicidal thoughts.

I was eighteen years old that summer, so I was the oldest person in the program. While this may seem like a setback for some, this really only launched me into a place of leadership. I was the oldest and I was respected. I took that seriously, just as I did my recovery. This meant I was not only supporting my peers, but I was also fully engaged in what I was learning during the day at the academic center associated with 2East. I had an educator at the academic center who taught me both elements of Cognitive Behavioral Therapy (CBT) and Dialectical Behavioral Therapy (DBT) to help aid my recovery. CBT is a therapy that helps people change patterns of thinking and feeling to ultimately change behavior. CBT is very effective for anxiety disorders, as well as for anyone looking to change behavior and thought patterns. CBT helped me challenge some of my core beliefs and helped me be honest in my treatment rather than striving to be "smiling and perfect." I also had an introduction to DBT during this time. DBT is a therapy created by Marsha Linehan. DBT is based in four modules, including (i) mindfulness, (ii) distress tolerance, (iii) interpersonal effectiveness and (iv) emotional regulation. During my time at the academic center, we learned about different aspects of each of the modules, specifically distress tolerance. Distress tolerance skills are very important for those who turn to any type of harmful behavior when in distress. Distress tolerance offers other suggestions for managing those urges and for taking the edge off the high intensity of emotions.

On the weekends, I went on "passes," which allowed me to leave the unit and practice what I was learning out in the world. When I was back on the unit during the week, I worked on deepening relationships with others and completing therapeutic homework from my educator at the academic center. One thing my educator pushed me to do was write a "life history." A "life history" is like a mini-memoir and is meant to be both empowering and enlightening. When I wrote my life history, I was able to look back at the early signs of my mental illness. I remember I had a few day counselors review it, and then I shared it with the community. When you shared your life history with the community at East House, it was an indicator that you had moved up a "level" in the program. Like many therapeutic programs, 2East at McLean ran on a level system. Everyone started at a Level 3, your life history got you to level 4, and practically no one ever got to Level 5.

However, in true Dayna fashion, I got to Level 5. This gave me the opportunity to run my own lessons for my peers. Gaining Level 5 helped me find my voice and, in turn, an untouched piece of myself—one that was genuinely passionate about social work. So much so, I decided I would change my major from secondary education to social work in the fall when I returned to PC. Just like my pursuit of becoming a teacher was inspired by my own experiences in middle school, pursuing social work was in large part inspired by Jackie. Jackie was a day counselor, specifically called a Community Residence Counselor (CRC) at McLean. Jackie started working at East House on my third day in the program, and I felt an immediate connection upon meeting her. I found it so easy to open up to Jackie. On the hardest nights, we played our favorite game, Bananagrams, to decompress. On the best nights, we celebrated. I would tell Jackie about my day in full review, and she would listen fully. She even got me a Friendly's ice cream cake the night before I left East House to commemorate my hard work and my nineteenth birthday, which was just three days later.

Leaving Jackie and leaving East House was heartbreaking, but at least I conquered and was done with mental health!! Or so I thought. I remember I went to Wildwood, New Jersey, the next week with my family. This was an annual trip, and I found the time to reflect. I just felt so grateful for East House, for Jackie, for Kathy, for my family. I even made Kathy a waxed version of my hand for her waiting room, as it was and still is always filled with beautiful art. During that vacation, I ran along the beach with the seagulls; life felt worth living in a way it never had; I couldn't wait to live it.

—-

Before I returned to PC, my dad gave me a part birthday and part back to school gift: a plastic toolbox from Home Depot. So many mental health professionals talk about building the number of "tools you have in your tool box," so this was my dad's way of reminding me I had gained so many from the summer. He encouraged me to put my worksheets from East House inside. I had DBT, I had CBT, I had Kathy, and I had a new mindset. He wanted me to hold onto that, even when the "high" from treatment cooled

✓ PREHEAT THE OVEN TO 350F

✓ BEGIN TO MAKE CAKE BY ADDING:
  1 CUP WATER
  1/3 CUP OIL
  3 EGGS

✓ MIX INGREDIENTS IN A BOWL

✓ BAKE FOR 18-20 MINUTES

✓ LET CAKE COOL.

BAKER'S NOTES

East House in my eyes. The place that I truly found my
voice for the first time.

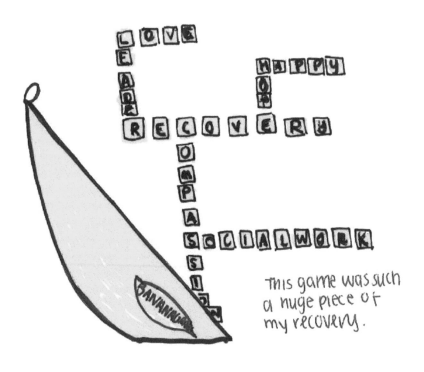

This game was such a huge piece of my recovery.

This was the exact moment I remember how happy I was to be alive. Running on the beach with the seagulls, August 2011, Wildwood NJ.

One of our favorite photo spots in Wildwood, NJ. An annual trip for the Altman family every August.

ONCE CAKE IS COOLED, CRUMBLE CAKE UNTIL IT RESEMBLES FINE CRUMBS

The first day of sophomore year at PC, I felt like a new confident woman. I was living in a tiny dorm room with two friends, consistently making lunch plans and attending parties. While I never drank at the parties, I loved that I had a social life. Drinking to me always felt like a total loss of control and something I wanted nothing to do with. I got comfortable saying no to alcohol, although I knew it would leave me out of experiences, I didn't want to lose control nor did I want to throw up; that was still very much on my mind. Nevertheless, I was proud of myself for having a "college experience" in addition to attending my new social work classes, which I loved. From "Intro to SWK" to "Gender Studies," I was proud of myself when I shared my mental health experiences in class. I felt like I held a unique perspective on therapy.

Plus, I was so excited that I would be making one of my ultimate dreams become a reality. "Changing the world," as broad and cliché as it sounds, has always been something I felt I was meant to do. I remember sitting at my dining room table after dinner in high school, making a list of things I could do to somehow make my mark. The way I was thinking about doing this changed in different life phases, from theater to visual art to dance. This time, though, it was through personal experience.

The summer of 2011 was impactful and changed me in so many ways, but one of the biggest was recognizing how many people live with eating disorders, self-hatred and/or body dissatisfaction. So, I decided to take action with my sister. Jamie, whom I never call Jamie (to me she is "babes," "bunny," "beans," "boo-boo"—anything endearing that starts with a "b") is three years younger than me and has always been the smartest and coolest person I know. Although we were close growing up outside of our typical sibling fights, my treatment was new territory for us. It felt hard for me to share with Jamie in a lot of ways. I wanted to protect her from my pain, and I think at the time I thought I was. Now, I know she was seeing it. How could she not have... she was living it with me.

Jamie had a similar hunger for changing the world and was always supportive in brainstorming with me at the kitchen table. She joined several of my endeavors, including a leading role in my performance group, "The Not So Off Broadway Players," when she was seven years old and I was ten. Jamie and I never really talked about the details of my eating disorder, but I knew the creation of "The BEA(YOU)TIFUL Project" was important to both of us.

"The BEA(YOU)TIFUL Project," formerly "The Beyoutiful Project" but I missed the memo when I set up the website, is a body positive and eating disorder awareness organization my sister and I started together in 2011. The organization started through our creation of handmade string bracelets, a means of connection we found when I was in treatment.

We started selling them online to support the National Eating Disorders Association (NEDA). We named the bracelets after people who inspired us, and it really took off. I was named a "PC Campus Celebrity," and we were featured in our hometown newspaper. We ended up selling hundreds of bracelets. I felt like I was making a difference, and this time it was by using my story. Advocacy became my passion, like an extension of the way creative projects always had been. My creative, entrepreneurial spirit was only enhanced by using my own story. I felt like an inspiration and, in a lot of ways, I was an inspiration. Throughout my semester, I continued to see the effects of my work on campus, and I was even asked to speak at events.

I am not sure if it was the public limelight that made it hard to admit I was struggling or the depth of my belief that I was only a good person if I appeared "happy"—but eventually things started to go downhill. I had not reached a point by any means to recognize I was in a position to show the world my authentic struggle within the project. I didn't know that eating disorder recovery usually comes with relapse. I didn't know that I could ask my psychiatrist to try a different medicine because my depression was getting worse, so I just kept smiling.

Things began to crumble in "fine crumbs" in every possible way. I thought the responsible thing to do was to ask Dr. M to seek treatment over winter break. She got scared and sent me to the emergency room to be evaluated. When I eventually saw the doctor at the ER, I was discharged, but part of me wanted help. I wanted to feel the way I felt at East House. I wanted to be that advocate again, the girl running on the beach with the birds in Wildwood, New Jersey. After the ER, Dr. M suggested I go back to McLean to have an intake for a partial program over winter break. The weekend before my intake appointment, where a professional would decide what program I should be put in, I went home to Southboro, and I was so depressed I created a plan to jump out of my bedroom window. I was so scared that my parents stayed with me that night, removing all sharp objects from my room and locking my window. When I went to the intake for the partial program at McLean the next day, I told the evaluator this, and she sent me to sit in a dark hallway. All I remember about that hallway was that the walls were beige and a man took my phone away. The evaluator told my mom to go home to get my things; I wouldn't be going anywhere. I got a hospital bracelet put on my wrist and I went to the second floor in an elevator to the Short Term Unit (STU).

Since I had turned nineteen the previous August, I was now being clinically treated as an adult, and this looked very different from being treated as an adolescent. I remember getting off the elevator and feeling scared. I saw people in hospital gowns, walking around aimlessly, looking like zombies. The staff were doing five-minute checks, in which they would locate each patient every five minutes and notate they were safe on a clipboard. I gave up the shoes I was wearing, as well as my sweatshirt and my belt. About an hour later, I remember my mom walking into the STU with my giant teddy bear. Everything was crumbling.

The first meal at the STU was the worst because I didn't know what to expect nor did I know anyone there. There were a few therapeutic group offerings, but practically no one attended. They were not required, and instead people stayed in their rooms, sleeping or reading. Some show about a taxi driver was on in the main room, all day. I didn't see my treatment team very often, especially since I had arrived right before Christmas and before a weekend. Doctors were on vacation, and I remember sitting in the phone booth calling home every day. My mom tried to be encouraging, but the most encouraging thing that happened to me during my stay was learning I might have Borderline Personality Disorder (BPD). Just like finding out there was a name for the anxiety I was feeling, BPD felt like the reason I was there. At first I felt relieved; maybe there was a cure for this, which there was not. But they told me about a type of therapy that could help, one that I had already been introduced to: Dialectical Behavioral Therapy (DBT). My mom ordered books on Amazon, and I was going to be officially screened for the disorder when I left the STU a few days later. My fourth and last night was the hardest. My next-door neighbor at the STU thought I was her daughter who had passed away. I was heartbroken for her, so I played along. I was scared of this woman, but mostly because I was scared I would become her. I'm honest, the five days I spent at the STU were five of the hardest days of my life. But as hard as it was, stabilization and inpatient units exist for a reason, and that is exactly where I needed to be.

✓ PREHEAT THE OVEN TO 350F

✓ BEGIN TO MAKE CAKE BY ADDING:
1 CUP WATER
1/3 CUP OIL
3 EGGS

✓ MIX INGREDIENTS IN A BOWL

✓ BAKE FOR 18-20 MINUTES

✓ LET CAKE COOL.

✓ ONCE CAKE IS COOLED, CRUMBLE CAKE UNTIL IT RESEMBLES FINE CRUMBS

BAKER'S NOTES

Finding my home and hugging my people in the first semester of Sophomore year at PC. This photo was taken in October 2011 on the night my sister and I launched "The BEA(YOU)TIFUL Project" website. I was met with such love and support during the launch! I am lucky to still be in touch with these friends, Sophia (left) and Mary (middle).

The official "About" photo for THE BEA(YOU)TIFUL Project website. This photo was taken at the end of the summer in Wildwood NJ,when we created the project officially. We were brainstorming on that trip actually. I was 19 and my sister was 16, Aug. 2011.

This giant Teddy Bear, Teddy, was given to me in February 2011. He became my confidant in treatment. This is a photo of us from vacation, but still felt relevant for this chapter.

ADD IN TWO CANS OF FROSTING TO THE BOWL OF FINE CRUMBS. ADD IN FROSTING A LITTLE BIT AT A TIME TO ENSURE YOU STILL HAVE A LITTLE CRUMBLE.

Upon leaving the STU, I was able to add some normalcy back into my life. That Christmas, I got the most beautiful jacket and screamed when I opened it. It was the purest joy I had felt since the semester started. I had professors waive my finals, and I even got a nice email from a PC friar whom I thought hated me. I started a partial program or "step down" for those who are at the STU, because it is hard to go from 24/7 structure to nothing. Although I had a car, my dad dropped me off every day. I was scared I would drive off the road if I ever hit the rock bottom place again. During the step down, I was screened for BPD, and while I did have traits, it was not enough to make a full diagnosis. Traits felt like enough though to feel like a failure. Though I learned there were several celebrities who were in the same spot, I felt unlovable. What does a borderline personality mean? I don't have a nice personality? And apparently, I don't have enough of it.

After leaving the step-down program, I went to Florida with my mom and my best friend at the time to continue to add in some "normalcy." Because I left the fall semester in crisis, going back to PC in the spring was still up in the air. I was required to have a re-entry meeting with my parents, the dean and Dr. M to ensure I could re-enroll as a full-time student. Not knowing if I could go back to school left me feeling scared. I always followed the path, so what would it mean if I did not go back to school? Had I failed? Those thoughts were too scary to even entertain, so I continuously reassured myself it wouldn't happen. Ultimately, the decision at the end of the re-entry meeting allowed for me to go back in the spring. I packed my duffle bag and arrived back on campus in Mid-January.

—-

About a week and a half into the semester, I lived one of the most pivotal days of my life. It was a Friday in late January. It was pouring outside, so I wore my black raincoat and black leggings to my Development of Western Civ class. Fridays were seminar class days for Development of Western Civ, and my seminar was held in Ray Dining Hall, since there were so few students. I sat down in my usual spot, and I flipped over a quiz grade waiting for me: a "52." An F? I got up before the class started and went to the bathroom. I went into the second stall and began to search and plot ways to end my life. I exited the stall for a strategy, and I caught myself in the mirror. Hysterically crying, I looked in the mirror and thought, "I know I don't want to feel this way anymore, but I am not totally sure I want to die in this bathroom." I called my mom, and she came to pick me up. I told my friends I was going home for the weekend. I didn't know what to do. Should I take a medical leave? That felt so "bad." What would I do? How could I not follow the path everyone else was on?

The next day was not any better, and I continued to fall apart. My dad encouraged me to call the hotline that was offered through McLean because I was once again in crisis. I remember calling and, automatically, my voice changed, once again masking how I felt. My dad grabbed the phone and squeezed my wrist so tightly, I was so scared. At that moment, we both knew I was taking a medical leave. I was crumbling again. That wasn't rock bottom before; I was falling another thousand feet.

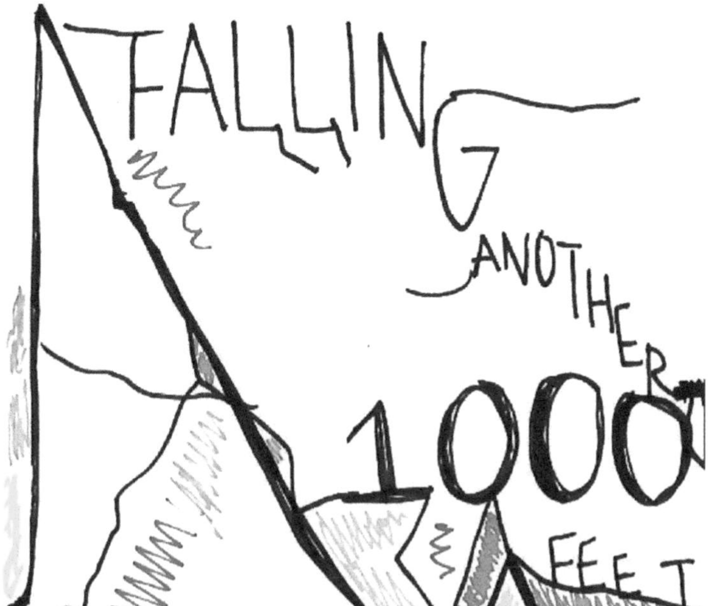
FALLING
ANOTHER
1000
FEET

✓ PREHEAT THE OVEN TO 350F

✓ BEGIN TO MAKE CAKE BY ADDING:
  1 CUP WATER
  1/3 CUP OIL
  3 EGGS

✓ MIX INGREDIENTS IN A BOWL

✓ BAKE FOR 18-20 MINUTES

✓ LET CAKE COOL.

✓ ONCE CAKE IS COOLED, CRUMBLE CAKE UNTIL IT RESEMBLES FINE CRUMBS

✓ ADD IN TWO CANS OF FROSTING TO THE BOWL OF FINE CRUMBS. ADD IN
  FROSTING A LITTLE BIT AT A TIME TO ENSURE YOU STILL HAVE A LITTLE
  CRUMBLE.

BAKER'S NOTES

USING AN ICE CREAM SCOOP OR SPOON, SCOOP TWO CAKE MIXTURE BALLS WORTH OF DOUGH AND ROLL IN A TIGHT BALL.

When I found out I was going on medical leave, the first thing my dad and I did was have lunch at Friendly's. I was relieved, but I also felt like the blank road ahead was overwhelming in itself. I felt guilty that I hadn't made the decision totally on my own, and I felt even worse about wanting to do nothing at all.

My therapist, Kathy, put me on the waiting list at the Hill Center at McLean Hospital, a program for women with depression, anxiety and trauma, and some with BPD. I continued to see Kathy weekly, but her mother died in the midst of our sessions. I was heartbroken for her and also unsure how to survive without therapy. Meanwhile my parents found the best psychiatrist they could in the state of Massachusetts to support this new diagnosis of traits: Dr. T.

Dr. T charged $300 for thirty minutes, and I very quickly realized how incredibly lucky and privileged I was, that my parents were not only willing but also had the means to let me see Dr. T bi-weekly. He started me on a new medicine "cocktail" and reassured me I would start to feel better.

There was a tightness in my chest over the coming months. My mom begged me to get a job, but I only lasted one shift in the one that I found. Most days, I couldn't get out of bed, and I didn't brush my teeth. I hardly showered, and I lived my life on my living room couch in a pink onesie. One of my parents had to stay home with me at all times, and I felt like the biggest burden to my family. My dad came home early from work most days, and we played Bananagrams on the dining room table. I was distraught over not being in school, but my dad reassured me that he didn't care if I mopped the floor at McDonald's, he just wanted me to be here.

I couldn't scoop myself up to do much of anything, and every day I prayed I would get off that waitlist for the Hill Center. But it was mid-February and still no phone call. I tried to start a blog documenting an activity for every day; I wanted a purpose. I didn't want to wait for things to get better. I couldn't see why they would. I even started volunteering at different organizations. I went to Roxbury twice a week to organize canned goods at a food pantry, and I served meals to men at a homeless shelter in Boston on the weekends. I always loved lifting other people up, and while the distraction was helpful in the moment, nothing truly changed.

Things continued to stay stagnant, so my mom suggested I try something new: taking ballet classes at the Boston Ballet School.

"Just try it," she begged me.

The day she planned on taking me, I ran behind the couch and yelled at her. I never yelled at my mom, ever. And she yelled back. She never yelled at me, ever. So, I scared myself enough to get in the car, and that was the best decision I could have made.

I took classes at least three times a week at the Boston Ballet School with a teacher named Helena. I never told Helena what I was going through, but consistently showing up to her class brought me light. So, did Ilyse. Ilyse is one of my cousin's best friends from college, who also took classes at the Boston Ballet School. She drove me there every day. Ilyse and I didn't talk about my mental health or what brought me to the Boston Ballet. We talked about dance and the hard grand-pliés Jonathan had us doing on Mondays. Ilyse, like Helena, played a significant role in my life without even knowing it.

I started to fall into a routine. My dad always picked me up from ballet, and we had lunch together at Roxy's Diner around the corner. I found my heart beating again in dance, and that expanded to my work on The BEA(YOU)TIFUL Project. I didn't want to leave it behind, so I didn't. My sister, Jamie, and I continued to make bracelets, and now we were starting a YouTube channel. Jamie was always talented at video editing. It was her idea to start building out a media component of the project, and it was beautiful. She put videos together to create hopeful montages. We had people messaging us on Facebook asking to be in our videos, and we even got some more publicity. This was great for me because I wanted nothing but to be discovered by Demi Lovato, my ultimate idol at the time, whom I saw going through exactly what I was. Not only do we have the same birthday, I felt connected to her by her struggles. I entered a writing contest and got to see her documentary premiere for *Stay Strong* at MTV Studios in New York City in early March. I remember watching her documentary like I was looking in the mirror. Everything she had been through with her own eating disorder treatment, self-harm, self-hatred... it was me. I felt an even greater sense of purpose when I saw the documentary. I reached out to more newspapers, online magazines and social media campaigns, any way to get The BEA(YOU)TIFUL Project message out even in the depths of my own despair.

As much as I felt I was unraveling, I was in a pretty good routine. It didn't mean that my pain went away, but I was surviving. I was doing what I could until I could go back to McLean. And as much as that day felt like it would never come, on March 29th, 2012, it did.

—-

Even though I had been to the hospital before, the night before my first day at the Hill Center at McLean, I watched a few YouTube videos to decide what to pack. I knew I would be staying there overnight as a part of their residential program, and I wanted to make sure I had what I needed. I knew I would be packing my new Boston Ballet fleece zip up jacket that got to the studio the night before. My mom gave a letter I wrote to Helena when she picked up the jacket, and while I never got a chance to see her again in person, I hoped that she would recognize what she did for me.

—-

When I woke up on March 29th, I threw my suitcase in the trunk of my mom's car and headed to the Hill Center bright and early. The Hill Center is one of the first visible buildings on the McLean campus, and as soon as I got there, I was pretty much thrown in. I fastened the lavender bow in my hair that matched my lavender striped shirt and took a deep breath. I didn't really know what to expect. After the first few groups in one main living room, we transitioned to the dining area for lunch. On my way over, I was pulled aside by my case manager.

"Hi, are you Dayna?"

 I smiled and nodded.

"Hi, I am Dena," she said. "I am going to be your case manager and I will come find you after lunch."

Lunch on that day felt endless. I remember texting my therapist, Kathy, feeling unable to breathe. I was so scared because all I wanted was this program, and here I was, afraid. She told me to knock on the staff door, because that's why I was there. I got up from my seat and knocked on the door where the staff were eating lunch, but my knock was too quiet and I went back to the dining room and started to cry.

The endless lunch finally wrapped up and I met with Dena. She took me to her office and I sat across from her on a comfortable couch. She pulled out some paperwork to go through: treatment plans, what goals we wanted to work on, paperwork for the insurance company. She started to ask me questions. I think the first one was as simple as "How old are you?" and I started to cry.

I vividly remember her trying to keep me on task while I was looking for the tissues. I kept telling her how I usually smile and don't cry when I meet people so this was a big deal, but she really wanted to just find out who I was before we dove any deeper. I was thrown off by this, Dena was tough. So, I texted Kathy to see if she thought I could ask for a different case manager. She encouraged me to stick it out. No one had really challenged me this way before and I was scared at first, but then I saw the value in it and my life changed forever.

Working with Dena became my favorite part of the Hill Center. I looked forward to seeing her every day. She was funny, and I recognized pretty quickly that she was one of the smartest people I had ever come in contact with. I couldn't believe how she was making connections from one part of my life to another seemingly out of nowhere. She held my heart close to her when we had difficult family meetings. She always situated my chair in the room close to hers when meeting with my family and would nod in my direction as a secret sign of support. Dena always believed in me, always. I had never really felt this before. She had unwavering faith in me and my abilities, and I tried very hard to borrow her perspective.

Throughout my time at the Hill Center, my life changed. I was reintroduced to Dialectical Behavioral Therapy (DBT), an approach I had learned about a year before at 2East. The Hill Center solely runs on DBT principles, so I was learning even more about the modules for coping. I found learning about Emotion Regulation at this time so helpful. I ran every community meeting at the center, and I found comfort in friends. I loved the day counselors: Vanessa, Kelsey, Haley. I felt important. I was so excited every morning when I saw Dena's car parked in the driveway from my window. She was teaching me how special I was without my eating disorder, without the bow in my hair and without being "nice"—just by being me.

On one of my last nights at the Hill Center, I was sitting on the floor of the living room working on "my crisis plan," an assignment Dena had given me before discharge. Around eight o'clock, I saw Dena come out of her office and walk by me to leave. I was shocked. 8:00 p.m.? Even though it was way after business hours and I am sure she had had a long day, she sat down next to me on the floor. I couldn't believe it; at 8:00 p.m.?! This moment solidified everything I had felt about her. Even though she reassured me she had *The Bachelor* taping at home, I knew then more than ever that she cared. She asked what I was doing, she was interested, and I felt so loved.

Upon my departure, I asked Dena if I could continue working with her as my DBT skills coach. I remember how nervous I was to ask her because I knew how much I wanted to keep our relationship in my life. I also wanted to keep working with my original therapist, Kathy, so we decided I would see Dena every other week as a skills coach. A few days after I was discharged from the Hill

Center, I got a large envelope in the mail welcoming me as a transfer student to Northeastern University. There was a part of me that didn't want to leave PC. I loved my friends, I loved knowing what I had there, but I was terrified of walking back into that dining hall bathroom and back into that place in my life. I didn't want to sit through another re-entry meeting. I needed a fresh start and my answer was in the form of a husky.

- ✓ PREHEAT THE OVEN TO 350F

- ✓ BEGIN TO MAKE CAKE BY ADDING:
  1 CUP WATER
  1/3 CUP OIL
  3 EGGS

- ✓ MIX INGREDIENTS IN A BOWL

- ✓ BAKE FOR 18-20 MINUTES

- ✓ LET CAKE COOL.

- ✓ ONCE CAKE IS COOLED, CRUMBLE CAKE UNTIL IT RESEMBLES FINE CRUMBS

- ✓ ADD IN TWO CANS OF FROSTING TO THE BOWL OF FINE CRUMBS. ADD IN FROSTING A LITTLE BIT AT A TIME TO ENSURE YOU STILL HAVE A LITTLE CRUMBLE.

- ✓ USING AN ICE CREAM SCOOP OR SPOON, SCOOP TWO CAKE MIXTURE BALLS WORTH OF DOUGH AND ROLL IN A TIGHT BALL.

BAKER'S NOTES

Going into Boston to volunteer during my medical leave was a way I tried to heal. I remember after organizing groceries at a food bank, I asked my mom to take this photo of me in the city. This photo was in honor of my favorite Demi Lovato song, "Skyscraper." This was a week before I was going to see her documentary in NYC called *Stay Strong.*

As residents of the Hill Center, we were asked to rotate who would cook dinner for the community. This is my friend, Amanda, and I trying to figure how to make Mac N' Cheese for all of the other patients. It didn't go well.

I smile when I look at this picture from April 2012. This was one of my last days at the Hill Center. My parents and I went to a park near the hospital and I felt like I was breathing again.

CONTINUE UNTIL ALL DOUGH IS ROLLED INTO TIGHT BALLS.

I continued to do what I needed to do before the fall 2012 move-in at Northeastern University (NU). I continued to see Kathy, Dena and Dr. T. I explored new career goals as an intern at the American Cancer Society and was interested in majoring in human services at NU. I had so much to be excited about when it came to transferring, but one source of relief was knowing most NU students complete five years of school because of the unique co-op program. I already knew I would be in school longer than my peers at PC since I took a medical leave, so I appreciated that I would not be alone in taking more time to graduate.

It was crazy for me to be in this place. I couldn't believe I had space to think about my career and going back to school, or really anything other than hating myself. I remember the excitement I felt when I went to transfer student orientation at NU—not only because I met potential friends but also because they had a bagel brunch. This was a big deal for my family. PC was a Catholic school, and while being Jewish at PC did not present too many challenges, I did feel left out at times. During my freshman year parents' weekend at PC, there was a brunch with no bagels. As Jews, we couldn't imagine a brunch without bagels, furthermore denoting that it was not the school for me. When I walked into the NU Curry Student Center with my parents and saw bagels during my NU orientation, we all felt like this was just "right."

And it was. I really enjoyed my classes, and I began to apply for student groups and clubs. I got into all of the student groups I applied for and became very involved in the Student Alumni Association (SAA) and Active Minds. As I continued to become comfortable, I told my friends and professors about The BEA(YOU)TIFUL Project and my lived experience with mental illness. I started speaking to campus sororities, creating workshops for young girls and telling my story.

As much as NU kept me "in tight" with myself, school continued to bring a lot of pressure. As hard as I worked to manage my anxiety, I still used grades as a way to measure my value. This was something I was used to doing, a core piece of my identity. Hard work was all that was acceptable and to me that meant 120 percent. As much as I was trying to break away from the pressure I put on myself, I remember during my first year at NU, I found out I had a 76 in a biology class and I was crushed. I felt the over-whelming panic in my chest, things became blurry, and before I knew it, I was running through Ruggles T station, the train station connecting one part of campus to my dorm. I was running away from failure, from the part of myself that still needed to be perfect. I took a breath and thought about how much I had to overcome to get to this place. There were times during my medical leave that I would have done anything to be back in school, even if that meant a C+. This perspective helped me catch my breath, and then I took out my phone to call Dena. She asked me what I thought I should do, and although I at first told her "I don't know…" I recognized I knew exactly what I needed to do, what had always helped: take action. So, I emailed my professor ask-ing what I could do to get my grade up. I called my friends to set up a time to go to Stetson West, our favorite dining hall. I knew at my core I wanted to be okay, I knew I wanted to recover, but above all else, I knew I wanted to continue.

—-

Over time my relationship with Dena grew, and I began seeing her weekly. Kathy remained, and still remains, one of the most impor-tant people in my life, but what I needed in that moment was Dena. Therapy with Dena became less about DBT skills and more about our relationship. I brought everything with me into the room, and so did she. At first, I started to write things down to guide our conversation, like an agenda, but eventually we got to know each other so well, we were in a great routine. So much so, she knew what I needed even just by the first words out of my mouth, and usually she told me to try saying it again, but without the "mask" or smile. Dena became maternal in so many ways. She made me peanut butter and jelly sandwiches, she cared about me unconditionally and I felt utterly loved for who I was. I began to let Dena see me, which meant absolutely no holding back. I didn't sit in therapy with a sweatshirt over my waist, body checking or half-listening, I was all in. And so was Dena. I also had the opportunity to watch Dena grow. I remember how intense she was when I first met her at the Hill Center, and I realized how much she softened in our work together. She even dropped that she had a boyfriend one time! I looked forward to seeing Dena every week. She was guiding me, I was doing the work and we became an absolutely unstoppable team.

✓ PREHEAT THE OVEN TO 350F

✓ BEGIN TO MAKE CAKE BY ADDING:
1 CUP WATER
1/3 CUP OIL
3 EGGS

✓ MIX INGREDIENTS IN A BOWL

✓ BAKE FOR 18-20 MINUTES

✓ LET CAKE COOL.

✓ ONCE CAKE IS COOLED, CRUMBLE CAKE UNTIL IT RESEMBLES FINE CRUMBS

✓ ADD IN TWO CANS OF FROSTING TO THE BOWL OF FINE CRUMBS. ADD IN
FROSTING A LITTLE BIT AT A TIME TO ENSURE YOU STILL HAVE A LITTLE
CRUMBLE.

✓ USING AN ICE CREAM SCOOP OR SPOON, SCOOP TWO CAKE MIXTURE BALLS
WORTH OF DOUGH AND ROLL IN A TIGHT BALL.

✓ CONTINUE UNTIL ALL DOUGH IS ROLLED INTO TIGHT BALLS

BAKER'S NOTES

As I began to become more comfortable using my voice, I found my passion for public speaking. I knew I loved being on stage from my early years in community theater but I had no idea how much it would mean to me to tell my own story in front of an audience. This picture is from the first large presentation I did at Northeastern. I practiced every day in front of my mirror for over a a month and I was so proud when I nailed it!

I found some of the most incredible friends through the Student Alumni Association at NU. I became very involved in the organization and eventually became the VP of Community Service for the club. We did several annual service events including Relay for Life.

"Again without the smile"

— Dena to Dayna
est. 2012

Dena always had me practice being authentic in our sessions.

To me PB&J meant
"I care about
you" ♡

It was a very
salient way to feel
Dena's "caring."
I smile when I
think of that☺

MELT TWO TO THREE OUNCES OF YOUR FAVORITE CHOCO-
LATE IN THE MICROWAVE.

2013: I was finally finding home at NU. I started off the new semester (and the new year) in my first co-op placement. The co-op
program at NU allows students to work in their field for six
months. Students "on co-op" do not take classes, and a lot of
times they get paid. Most co-op placements last about six
months, so needless to say on my first co-op, I was so excited to
be completely immersed in the human services field. My first
placement was at the Walker Home and School: a school and
residence for young children and adolescents who struggle with
their behavioral health. Just like one would apply for a job, I applied and interviewed for several co-op positions. I remember after my interview at Walker, I was asked to come back and ob-
serve for the day: This was the moment I knew I would take the
job. Being at Walker felt a lot like McLean, where I dreamed of
working after graduation. I remember vividly, the day I observed,
one of the residents asked if I would play Bananagrams with her,
the game I played almost every night with Jackie at East House
just a few years prior. I just knew this was the place.

Working at Walker though proved very challenging. I worked with
kids who were between the ages of four and nine years old. I
never saw myself working with this age group, so I had to adapt
quickly. I also got physically hurt quite often, which felt morally
and physically terrible. I did meet some great colleagues turned
friends though. On Wednesdays, we all went to a local bar to un-
wind, and on the weekend, it was either into the city to shop or
jumping on the trampolines at Skyzone. As hard as the work was,
I felt a part of something, and I felt connected.

I ended up going back to the Hill Center for a quick brush up during the end of my time at Walker. Dena could see I was slowly
melting away (both physically and emotionally), and she wanted
to get ahead of it. We both also felt I would get so much out of
the program if I wasn't truly in crisis. It was during this time that I
saw a new psychiatrist at McLean who suggested I did not have a
BPD diagnosis, in part due to a lack of traits. Dena and I further
discussed this, and it did feel like I was moving away from the
traits that were once associated with the disorder. I had not self-

harmed in years, and we got to know my suicidal thoughts serving a different purpose than those with BPD. I also worked toward entering relationships differently, and I began to see that I was outgrowing negative interpersonal patterns. For example, Dena helped me express my needs more clearly and helped me recognize the important role boundaries play in a relationship. Growing up, I was afraid of boundaries, not only at home but also with friends. After my experience in middle school, I feared boundaries would interfere with connection or closeness in a relationship, but I had worked to realize it was just the opposite. I found that healthy relationships are truly preserved by them. The hard work felt good. Not just in therapy but in my everyday life. I used this time at the Hill Center to reflect and move forward. My case manager this time, Amy, helped me do that. We used mindfulness, one of the core principles of DBT, often in our sessions. I really liked Amy; she had a great sense of humor and a ton of photos on her wall, and she introduced me to new ways DBT could be helpful. I left the Hill Center for the second time hoping it would be the last, and I am happy to say, so far it has been.

—-

When the fall semester started, I was back in classes after my co-op at Walker, and I never felt better. Things felt so normal, I began thinking about my future. One day, I sat in Dena's office and told her I was thinking about going on Birthright. Birthright is an opportunity for people who are Jewish and between the ages of eighteen and twenty-six to go to Israel for free for ten days. Being Jewish was always important to me, especially because of Grandpa Michael. Grandpa Michael was actually my great grandfather, and we had a close relationship. He loved being Jewish and I loved him. He played a huge role in my mom's life and it was important to her that we remained close. I knew how much he wanted me to experience Israel. I cherished our relationship. I have such fond memories of going to visit him in Florida, spending the day at the pool and then going out to dinner at 3:45 p.m. to beat "the rush."

With Grandpa Michael, my family and Dena on board, I was ready to sign up. My biggest hesitation at that point was the long plane ride, but my psychiatrist, Dr. T., gave me some suggestions of what could ease my anxiety on the plane.

—-

I met the group of people I would be traveling with at the JFK International airport in New York City on December 18, 2013. I clicked pretty quickly in the airport with two guys I recognized from the pre-departure meetings. The three of us were the first to arrive, so we got to talking. One of them was especially cute, and I kept my eyes on him all the way to Jerusalem. I fantasized about him until day two when he shared that he was gay, and then his friend became more of the romantic interest. His friend was hot, but *like way* out of my league. He found out that I was interested in him, and he quickly took advantage of that in every way. He was manipulative and mean. He got angry when I didn't do what he wanted. It was hard to move away from him on the bus or during the day in our activity groups. He touched me in public places, and I hated that. I continuously said no and he didn't listen. One day after a hike in the Golan Mountains, he asked me if I would go back to his room "to make out, that's it," and he raped me. During the experience, he kept yelling at me to open my eyes, but I couldn't. I didn't want to believe it was real. He wouldn't let go of me, until I finally told him I had to go to the bathroom so badly, I was going to pee on him. He was grossed out enough that he relinquished me from his grip. I ran to the bathroom and began to run the water from the faucet so I could let the tears fall from my eyes, but they didn't. I left the bathroom and picked my clothes up off the floor. Before I left, he asked who else he thought was interested in him. He also asked how I felt he compared to the other guys on the trip and how many girls he could "get" before we went back to the U.S. I told him everything he wanted to hear, and I walked back to my own room on the kibbutz.

When I got to my room on the kibbutz, there were a few girls sitting on my roommate's bed. The moment I walked in, they quickly asked me what was wrong. I couldn't really articulate anything that had just happened, and what they did get from me was that it was a bad experience. They reassured me that it gets easier when you are more sexually experienced. They all left to go to

83

dinner, and I didn't know what to do. I decided to take a shower, to melt everything away. I turned up the water temperature as high as it could go, but it was freezing. Living on a kibbutz or a community farm in Israel, there is only so much hot water for the community. I was desperate to get him off of me though, even if it meant I was taking an ice bath. The freezing cold water left bumps on my skin. I got myself together after the shower, I remember saying to myself as I walked out the door, "You only have a few more days, then you can go home and explode." I walked aimlessly to the dining center at the kibbutz; everything was such a blur—a man in a golf cart approached and asked me if I wanted a ride to dinner. I got in... What could be worse than what had just happened?

The following days, I lived in a haze. I wish I had advocated to leave the trip early, but instead I smiled and nodded my way through the rest of our days in Israel. I tried to reach out to the trip leaders to talk about what had happened, but without the language, and with the mere fact that I was traumatized, I hesitated and froze; I just did not know what to say. One of the last nights in the desert, rumors began to circulate about how terrible I was in bed. It didn't help that these rumors coincided with the night we (all forty of us) would all be sharing a tent together. I begged my friends on the trip not to tell the leaders. My friends wanted to make sure he was being held responsible for what he did and ultimately get him kicked off the trip, but I was so scared of him. What would he do if I upset him? Something worse?

Ten days later, I ran off the plane, an emotional mess, arriving back to the United States. I got my luggage, got in the car and immediately told my mom what happened. She told me something similar had happened to her, which was truly not what I wanted to hear in the moment. I felt my experience was inferior or that it didn't matter. I was left feeling bad for my mom. A few days later, I tried to tell Dena what happened, but I immediately shut down when she didn't respond the way I had hoped. My words melted, my emotions melted, I melted, until there was nothing left. I started my second co-op at Boston Children's Hospital in January 2014. This was a dream placement for me, but I felt like I was sleepwalking through the first few months. Everything that I worked for I felt was gone. I felt so numb, I would wash my hands with burning hot water and lie on my apartment floor and cry for hours. I got text messages from my perpetrator apologizing, but I told him it was okay. I had no respect for myself anymore, feeling I somehow deserved it; I was deep in shame and self-hatred.

In the coming months, I extended my hours at Boston Children's Hospital. Going home after my shift was the worst thing I could do since it meant I was left alone with my thoughts. Little did I know my change in hours meant that I crossed over with Caroline. Caroline was the night manager of the program we worked in, and someone I still consider a great friend. I eventually opened up to her about being sexually assaulted, and just having that one person listen changed the way I validated this for myself. She sat with me while I blocked my perpetrator's phone number. She hugged me and told me it would be okay. This shifted my healing. I began to think about what had helped me at rock bottom before. Of course, my support system, but also advocacy: The BEA(YOU)TIFUL Project. I thought about how much I was helped by using my story to make it "okay" for others to share theirs. Although I wasn't ready to talk about what had happened to me, yet, I was ready to be an advocate. I watched *Law and Order: SVU* every night once I decided I would take a stand for survivors of sexual violence. I wanted to be the non-detective version of Olivia Benson, the main character in the show, investigating sex crimes and helping victims find their power in their stories. Olivia, but moreover, the actress who plays her, Mariska Hargitay, tells survivors what they went through matters... they matter. I wanted to be that, even if I wasn't able to give that to myself yet.

✓ PREHEAT THE OVEN TO 350F

✓ BEGIN TO MAKE CAKE BY ADDING:
  1 CUP WATER
  1/3 CUP OIL
  3 EGGS

✓ MIX INGREDIENTS IN A BOWL

✓ BAKE FOR 18-20 MINUTES

✓ LET CAKE COOL.

✓ ONCE CAKE IS COOLED, CRUMBLE CAKE UNTIL IT RESEMBLES FINE CRUMBS

✓ ADD IN TWO CANS OF FROSTING TO THE BOWL OF FINE CRUMBS. ADD IN
  FROSTING A LITTLE BIT AT A TIME TO ENSURE YOU STILL HAVE A LITTLE
  CRUMBLE.

✓ USING AN ICE CREAM SCOOP OR SPOON, SCOOP TWO CAKE MIXTURE BALLS
  WORTH OF DOUGH AND ROLL IN A TIGHT BALL.

✓ CONTINUE UNTIL ALL DOUGH IS ROLLED INTO TIGHT BALLS

✓ MELT TWO TO THREE OUNCES OF YOUR FAVORITE CHOCOLATE IN THE
  MICROWAVE.

BAKER'S NOTES

The drawing contains handwritten text: "a am enough", "overcome", "this may be starting to get excessive...?", "#bracelets #inspiration", "May 22, 2013"

I was constantly adding bracelets to my left wrist. This is a drawing of one of my instagram posts in May 2013.

Welcoming 2013 with some of my best friends (from left): Gillian, me, Nicole and Alyssa. We were ready for the new year and I was excited to be welcoming it with my new found routine and mindset.

One of the most important branches of The
BEA(YOU)TIFUL Project was the work that we did
with young girls. My sister, Jamie and I, as the
founders held workshops at Young Women's Con-
ferences. Jamie missed this event because she
was at college in New York at the time, so I
brought along my friend, Allie (in the bottom right
corner). This was from a workshop we ran at the
Young Women's Conference in Plymouth NH.

This is Grandpa Michael with his daughter, my Grandma Leslie, and me. This picture is from one of my trips to Florida and was absolutely taken during a dinner that occured (I am sure) before 4PM. My mom and I would go to Florida together to visit them. I miss Grandpa Michael so much since he passed away in 2014.

This is a picture from one of my first days on Birthright. This was taken in Haifa.

DIP THE TIP OF THE CAKE POP STICKS INTO THE CHOCOLATE
AND INSERT INTO THE CAKE BALLS ABOUT HALFWAY.

I began to dip the tips of my toes back into advocacy when I
started my second organization, entitled "Erasing Excuses." This
was a photoblog that I began in the Boston community. I walked
around Boston with a whiteboard and asked strangers to think of
excuses we give perpetrators of sexual violence. I took a picture.
Then I had them "erase the excuse" they wrote on the whiteboard
and write a rebuttal statement. I took a second picture. I put the
pictures next to each other in blog form. I got other friends to do
this, and then it expanded to a community-wide movement. I was
inserting myself back into the advocacy world, and that truly
helped me heal. I also began opening up more to Dena in therapy.
She let me be angry with her for her response and for misunder-
standing. She invited me to talk about what I would have wanted
from her and how it was hard to not have had it. She encouraged
me to hold onto the idea that this trauma would be a "piece of my
quilt" and not the whole quilt someday. It was so hard to believe
her, but I wanted to. I told her my story over and over again until it
began to feel somewhat okay. We identified stuck points in the
story, and then I told it again. And again. Outside of therapy, I became connected to other people in the advocacy community, including one of my mentors, Mark.

I met Mark when he came to speak in one of my classes at NU
about his involvement with the Joyful Heart Foundation (JHF).
JHF was started by Mariska Hargitay, *Law and Order: SVU's*
Olivia Benson herself(!!), after she recognized the extent and
reach of the issues of domestic violence, sexual assault and child
abuse through her role on the show. She felt she had to do something to transform the way society saw these issues and end violence once and for all. I wanted to support JHF from the moment
I learned about it. I saw JHF as a way to make change on an even
bigger scale. I was always so inspired by Mariska, and I imagined
what it would be like to meet her one day.

After meeting Mark in my class, we had coffee and I told him
about all of my ideas. Little did he know, I was ready to insert my
passion and commitment to the Joyful Heart Foundation in total
solidarity right away. I sprung into action mode yet again. My sis-

ter, one of my best friends, Gillian, and I created a PSA video to support JHF the following week.

A few months later, I continued this momentum. I collaborated with another NU student and the two student groups I was very involved with—Active Minds and the Student Alumni Association, (SAA)—to create an event entitled "I See, I Speak, I Pledge." This was an event to encourage students to commit to speaking up and taking action if they witnessed or heard about sexual violence of any kind. The day of the event, there were workshops and teal balloons, resource tables and t-shirts. The day was so special to me: I made new connections on campus, I felt like a leader and it was the first time my new boyfriend, J, met my parents.

J and I met through our involvement in a student organization, Active Minds. Active Minds is a national nonprofit organization dedicated to changing the conversation around mental health, specifically for college students. J had his own relationship with mental health, both personally and within his family. I felt like he really "saw" me. He already knew that mental health was important to me, as I helped found the Active Minds chapter at NU and was the current vice president. I also was very upfront with him about my story. I didn't want him to be "partially inserted" into my life; I wanted all in. We started dating that April.

—-

I remember leaving J's apartment one day in May and getting a call from Dena. I was surprised. Dena lets me call and text her if I need to outside of our appointments, but this felt odd. I skeptically answered the phone thinking it was a misdial, but she told me she had a cool opportunity for me. Every year, McLean Hospital has an annual dinner to both fundraise and celebrate the mission of the hospital. They were looking for "survivor" stories and my name surfaced. Without hesitating, I knew what came next: I screamed "YES!" I wanted to do it, whatever "it" meant. I came to find "it" was sharing the story of my recovery in a video. Both Dena and I were interviewed on camera to talk about my growth and the way McLean influenced my life. As much as I could not wait to share my story, Dena was continuously careful that I felt "seen" through the process. She didn't want me to feel like a poster child for the hospital rather an individual. Although her concerns were valid, this is not how I saw it. McLean was the place I got my life back and where I learned to live in a new way; I wanted to share.

—-

Two weeks before the dinner, I sat in Dena's office, showing her pictures of two potential dress options.

"Should I wear the one with the pastel colors or just a black dress?"

Dena looked distracted. I could tell there was something she wasn't saying. She glanced away for a moment and then excitedly said, "Well I know I need to go shopping for the dinner, because I am pregnant!" My heart dropped. I was, of course, happy for her, but what did that mean for us? Not just would she come back after maternity leave, but what did this mean for our relationship?

I was really upset with myself for not being able to be totally excited for her, but I was scared. After the dinner I would be going to Germany and Poland for five weeks for a shortened study abroad program through NU. Five weeks... wow... I knew she could look totally different when I came back.

Regardless, I put this to the side for the annual dinner, and it was truly one of the best nights of my life. A month before, I had been invited to a similar gala for the Joyful Heart Foundation by my mentor Mark. It was star studded, inspirational and beautiful, and I felt the McLean Dinner would be similar. In many ways, it was! While there was not a red carpet, there were passed appetizers and celebrities. After they played the video and recognized my hard work in recovery, I was introduced to Jane Fonda and Maya Rudolph. Maya Rudolph told me I inspired her when I nervously asked her for a picture. Jane Fonda was also supportive, but she told me she liked my hair better curly. It was weird, but honestly it didn't matter; I felt like the celebrity... People were lining up to talk to me! They were so inspired by my story, and I just remember every moment I was hanging onto so tight. Additionally, Dena got to meet J that night, whom I had now been dating for several months. It meant a lot to me to have them meet. I said goodbye to Dena that night and saw her again in person in August when I arrived back from Germany.

- ✓ PREHEAT THE OVEN TO 350F

- ✓ BEGIN TO MAKE CAKE BY ADDING:
  1 CUP WATER
  1/3 CUP OIL
  3 EGGS

- ✓ MIX INGREDIENTS IN A BOWL

- ✓ BAKE FOR 18-20 MINUTES

- ✓ LET CAKE COOL.

- ✓ ONCE CAKE IS COOLED, CRUMBLE CAKE UNTIL IT RESEMBLES FINE CRUMBS

- ✓ ADD IN TWO CANS OF FROSTING TO THE BOWL OF FINE CRUMBS. ADD IN FROSTING A LITTLE BIT AT A TIME TO ENSURE YOU STILL HAVE A LITTLE CRUMBLE.

- ✓ USING AN ICE CREAM SCOOP OR SPOON, SCOOP TWO CAKE MIXTURE BALLS WORTH OF DOUGH AND ROLL IN A TIGHT BALL.

- ✓ CONTINUE UNTIL ALL DOUGH IS ROLLED INTO TIGHT BALLS

- ✓ MELT TWO TO THREE OUNCES OF YOUR FAVORITE CHOCOLATE IN THE MICROWAVE.

- ✓ DIP THE TIP OF THE CAKE POP STICKS INTO THE CHOCOLATE AND INSERT THEM INTO THE CAKE BALLS ABOUT HALFWAY. THIS WILL SECURE THEM THROUGH THE PROCESS

BAKER'S NOTES

This is one of the first photos that I took as part of Erasing Excuses. I don't think I even know this man's name but he very quickly became the face of the project after I met him on the streets of Boston. I loved the message he wrote and I will always stand behind it.

I made one of my first videos for Erasing Excuses a few months into the project. Although I do not drink, I know alcohol can play a role in incidents of sexual violence (especilly on college campuses).

"Being drunk" in and of itself is an excuse rape culture gives perpetrators but it is never an excuse to defend behavior or a means to victim blame.

This was the ultimate moment I met my hero, Mariska Hargitay. She will always be the person I look up to as I truly feel she uses her "power" for "good." People know, trust and love Mariska so they listen to her. And, we are so lucky to have someone like Mariska to listen to. The work she does to empower survivors on and off the screen is admirable to say the least. I will always want to make change and impact the world the way she does. This was an unforgettable night in May 2014.

This was the first photo taken at the McLean Annual Dinner on June 20, 2014 and it was with both Jane Fonda and Dena! If you look closely, you can see Dena has a bracelet on her wrist that says "Brave." I made this for her in honor of the song we chose to have played in the background of our video: "Brave" by Sara Bareilles.

I believe Maya Rudolph will always be one of the most
down to earth celebrities I will ever meet. She told me I
was an inspiration after watching my video at the
McLean Annual Dinner and I could really not be smiling
any bigger in this photo. Thank you, Maya!

Oh what to say Dena, other than thank you for being everything you are. You mean more to me than I
could ever express.

A few days after the Annual Dinner at McLean Hospital, I went to Germany and Poland with other students from NU to study Genocide through the lens of the Holocuast. The entire trip was incredibly moving and emotional, but we did enjoy our time there as well. This was the night Germany won the World Cup in 2014. We were in Berlin that night, it was amazing to feel a part of history.

FREEZE DOUGH BALLS FOR 20 MINUTES

When I saw Dena for the first time upon my arrival back into the U.S., I realized just how badly I wished I hadn't left. I knew it was only a matter of weeks until she would be going on maternity leave, and I didn't know what I was going to do internally. Externally, things were taken care of. I was going to see Amy, Dena's colleague from the Hill Center that I briefly worked with, but internally I was worried about what would happen to us.

These worries came earlier than I thought, as Dena was out earlier and longer than expected. I saw Amy through the fall of my senior year of college. I was still dating J, and I was loving my fall classes and executive board roles in both Active Minds and SAA.

I yearned to continue to freeze time as I entered my second semester of my senior year of college. I loved my roommates, my friends, my time at NU and my life. In February 2015, I created one of the most meaningful projects I am convinced I will ever create. This was an event called "Fashion in Action'' (FIA). FIA was completely me. Up until this point, I always had someone co-collaborating with me. As much as I had the ideas and the passion, I was scared to step outside the shadow of a second person to create, but for this one, I was ready to be fully responsible and do this on my own. FIA was a fashion show that benefited rape crisis and domestic violence shelters across Massachusetts. Over the months of December and January, I collected over nine-hundred pieces of donated clothing from the community. I went through the clothes every night while watching *Law and Order: SVU*. I had friends come over on snow days to help make outfits that would be modeled down the runway. I organized and rehearsed with models, I found a DJ, and there were acapella groups and spoken word poets for entertainment that night as well. I charged admission to support the Joyful Heart Foundation, and someone from the organization in NYC even came to speak. After the fashion show, all of the modeled clothing and the hundreds of other pieces were donated to rape crisis and domestic violence shelters across the state. It was one of my proudest accomplishments, and not just because it was very successful, but because I did it on my own.

I woke up the morning after Fashion in Action and felt what I would imagine hungover to feel like. I went to see Dena the following Monday, and she told me she had some news. She was moving to St. Louis. Her husband got a job there, and the family would be moving in about two weeks. I think my jaw dropped, and for those two weeks I was heartbroken. She offered to Skype with me for appointments but I was hesitant; I couldn't imagine how that would even work. Instead, two weeks later during our final session, she gave me a mug that said "You are So Loved." This mug, which sits in the cup holder of my car to this day, made the move feel okay. I knew even if Dena wasn't in my life every week, I would be with her, and I had never felt like this before. I feared my whole life being forgotten, and here was the moment, things were changing. I was scared, but when I walked out of that office holding the mug, I knew it wasn't over; I knew I would continue to be important to Dena. She taught me so much.

—-

The next months flew by, and before I knew it, I was taking the "T" with two of my best friends to the Boston TD Garden to graduate (with honors) from Northeastern University. I utterly could not believe it, and neither could my parents. High school graduation felt like something everyone did, but college—this was special. There were so many moments between September 2010 to this moment in May 2015 that had made me feel I would never see this day, but it was here. I had tears in my eyes for most of the ceremony, and so did my parents. We got to celebrate with J at The Capital Grill afterwards, and it didn't even feel real. I remember going to sleep that night in the bed I grew up in my parents' house. I had cried myself to sleep so many nights in that bed. I had several panic attacks in that bed, and now I was looking at my college diploma in that bed. That would be the moment I would freeze.

✓ PREHEAT THE OVEN TO 350F

✓ BEGIN TO MAKE CAKE BY ADDING:
1 CUP WATER
1/3 CUP OIL
3 EGGS

✓ MIX INGREDIENTS IN A BOWL

✓ BAKE FOR 18-20 MINUTES

✓ LET CAKE COOL.

✓ ONCE CAKE IS COOLED, CRUMBLE CAKE UNTIL IT RESEMBLES FINE CRUMBS

✓ ADD IN TWO CANS OF FROSTING TO THE BOWL OF FINE CRUMBS. ADD IN
FROSTING A LITTLE BIT AT A TIME TO ENSURE YOU STILL HAVE A LITTLE
CRUMBLE.

✓ USING AN ICE CREAM SCOOP OR SPOON, SCOOP TWO CAKE MIXTURE BALLS
WORTH OF DOUGH AND ROLL IN A TIGHT BALL.

✓ CONTINUE UNTIL ALL DOUGH IS ROLLED INTO TIGHT BALLS

✓ MELT TWO TO THREE OUNCES OF YOUR FAVORITE CHOCOLATE IN THE
MICROWAVE.

✓ DIP THE TIP OF THE CAKE POP STICKS INTO THE CHOCOLATE AND INSERT
THEM INTO THE CAKE BALLS ABOUT HALFWAY. THIS WILL SECURE THEM
THROUGH THE PROCESS

✓ FREEZE FOR 20 MINUTES

BAKER'S NOTES

Feb. 17, 2015: The most beautiful gift, my last session with Dena [in person].

During my fifth and final year at NU, I was in Executive Board roles in both clubs I dedicated myself to over my time at Northeastern. This is a photo from National Suicide Prevention Day. As the Vice President of Active Minds at NU, we had a table with resources and information to encourage students to ask for help.

As I felt more and more like myself during my final
year of college, I was able to deepen friendships,
even ones that I had for a long time. These are
my best friends from High School and we only
grew closer through college and beyond. From
the bottom this is: Nicole, me, Gillian and Alyssa.

The moment I had the idea to pursue Fashion in Action, I knew it was going to be big. But 950 pieces of clothing big? I am not so sure. This was after the first round of collecting clothing from the community. I organized it all by category and then by size. Although it was time consuming, it was an amazing process!

February 12, 2015: the night of Fashion in Action! This is a photo of me along with Paws, the NU Mascot and the women who modeled the clothing in the show!

From left to right: Gabi, Emily, Christina and I were roommates during our last year of college. The three of them were friends before and I was put in their apartment randomly! We lived on the sixteenth floor of the most beautiful apartment building on campus, one of the nicest apartment buildings I will probably ever live in. These girls welcomed me with open arms and I am so lucky to be their friend. Since graduating, we have stayed close and in touch over the years. We all saw Christina get married in June 2019 and made sure we stayed connected and entertained through Zoom during COVID-19.

This is one of my favorite photos of all time. I remember how genuinely happy I felt in that moment. This was taken the night of graduation at The Capital Grille to celebrate my accomplishment, taken May 2015!

Three days after graduation, I walked into my first day at my dream job: McLean Hospital. I was working as a Community Residence Counselor on a similar unit to East House. I had been preparing for this day since I left 2East. This was all that I wanted— the opportunity to make a difference in the lives of those who were feeling just like me. During my last two years of college, I took a yellow piece of construction paper and made a flag that said "MCLEAN" and stuck it to my wall. It was all that I worked for that whole time, and it was coming true.

Preparing doesn't always mean perfection though. In fact, I tested positive for latent tuberculosis (TB) on my first day. Believe it or not, many people have latent tuberculosis and don't even know it, but if you do, it usually means you can't work in the healthcare industry unless you begin a nine-month period of heavy medication. Without hesitation, I filled the prescription, but I got very sick —not only physically: it also affected my mental health. The medication was so strong, it totally shut down my body, and it was suggested that I cut down on one of my medications to make sure my body would be able to handle the nine-month dosage. At first Dr. T was hesitant. I think he was worried that I was overreacting to some of the things I had googled. I mean, I knew he was the doctor, but I was scared that the medication was going to make me more depressed or gain weight. I was so scared of ever hitting rock bottom again, I decided to cut the pills in half myself. I had never done this before, and I will never do it again. After a week of managing my own medication, I realized just how much I needed the full dosage. I felt its effects most amplified when traveling to Las Vegas for a family wedding. I can vividly remember it being hard for me to even get out of the bed in the hotel room without crying. I was so irritable, which only activated my anxiety. I obsessed over the same thought over and over again. I realized that this was due not only to not taking the full dose of medication but also because things were complicated by beginning sessions with a new therapist, Dr. P.

Dr. P and I first met during my medical leave. During the last month of waiting to get into the Hill Center, I joined a DBT therapeutic group she was facilitating. When Dena left, I thought resuming therapy with Dr. P was a safe choice. She knew me already, and I would not have to start completely over with someone else. I knew that Dr. P was well respected in her field, but I never left a session with her feeling better; instead I left feeling only worse. In the beginning of our work together, I felt she went out of her way to support me in a few phone sessions when I found out I had tested positive for latent TB. As a thank you, I spent a few hours painting her a canvas. When I gave it to her, I could tell it was going to be a problem. Many therapists feel uncomfortable with gift giving, but that was something I wouldn't have known. She gave it back to me and said, "This isn't a gift, this is a 'don't forget about me.'" I was confused; I really did think it was a gift. As hard as I tried to understand her perspective, I felt she didn't hear me. This started the first of many sessions that felt more punitive than therapeutic, to the point that I thought about self-harming again to manage the pain that was increased by Dr. P.

It has taken me a long time to process this part of my treatment journey because it was truly painful. However, if anything, I believe it gave me a better understanding of how hard therapy is when it is not the right therapist. I had such amazing relationships with Kathy and Dena, I didn't completely know how hard therapy could be if you were sitting with someone who didn't "see you" or support you. I felt Dr. P didn't see me as a person, she saw me as a diagnosis, and that hurt in so many ways.

Things were feeling similarly uncomfortable in Dr. T's office. Dr. T and Dr. P knew each other well, and he was having a hard time imagining me having a negative experience with Dr. P. At that point, I felt like I didn't matter to either of them at all.

During that summer, I asked Dr. T if I could be evaluated for Obsessive-compulsive disorder (OCD). I had been using compulsions to manage my anxiety my whole life, and honestly it was so normal for me. From the routines I created in elementary school to the ten pencils on my desk before a test and the vomit phobia, I never really thought these things could be part of a larger diagnosis... for so long they were just "me."

I asked him twice to be screened for OCD, and both times he was very dismissive and refused. He told me he would not put me on another medication, which really was not what I was looking for; rather, I was looking for a different one, a new outlook, but he shut me down. Overwhelmed with emotion, I didn't know what to do. I didn't feel like anyone really "got me," so I decided to call the person who did.

I wasn't prepared for the flood of emotions that came back when I called Dena. She sounded happy, like things were going well in St. Louis, and she was proud of me for calling her. I remember going down the stairs of my parents house (where I was living while working at McLean), smiling after our conversation. My dad asked me what was going on and I told him I had talked to Dena. He said to me: "Why don't you just try Skyping with her? After all, Dena is your girl!!"

So, the next week, Dena and I began again but through Skype. At first it was hard; a lot of time had passed and without even realizing it, opening up to Dena in the way I had before was scary for me. Working at McLean also presented some new challenges. Being a patient at McLean and working there were very different. I think when I was a patient, I saw the hospital through "rose-colored glasses," and while I absolutely love and respect that hospital, as an employee, I saw the more "human side" of the institution. This was the side that was imperfect, just like the different personalities that come with every workplace, and at times it was difficult for me to connect back to why I was there in the first place. It was hard not to feel overwhelmed at times or jaded in some way, and I hated that. I knew I wanted to be at McLean, helping teens with all of me, but it felt unattainable a lot of the time.

About a year into working as a community residence counselor or "floor staff," I applied and was promoted into a new position on the unit: a DBT educator. Like many programs I attended through McLean, this one was DBT-based. As an educator, I was with the teens during the day to teach them the different modules and practices of the therapy. I dove back into finding true value in DBT, and I even had my own classroom. I really thrived in this role and connected deeply with many of the teens that I had the privilege to teach. It was important to me that the teens I taught were engaged and invested. Even if this meant that some days I let them have a talent show in the class or did a cartwheel to make a point of the importance of the skill "opposite action." I felt and still feel that life should feel accessible to everyone. DBT is a therapy with several modules, skills and practices, but one of the most salient goals of the therapy is to help those who struggle to "build a life worth living." And as an educator, I felt like I was doing this in the truest sense.

Even as an educator though, working at McLean brought more challenges than I expected. Not to mention, being out of college left me feeling both disconnected and bored, so I searched for new outlets. First it was art. I have always loved painting and drawing, but that is not an area of natural talent for me, to say the least, so I moved onto Zumba. Exercise historically scared me, as I always connected to it in the way I saw my eating disorder, but I loved the community I found in the studio.

When I was not Zumba-ing or teaching, I was planning and preparing my next project. I wanted to continue to create, to advocate and to make change, but it was hard. I did not have the built-in audience that I had at NU, nor the time and energy I did when I was in classes. My well-meaning family suggested I just watch TV, but that was never the way I did things.

During one session I had with Dena, we started to talk about life after McLean. This felt so hard, because when I started, I had truly felt I would be at McLean until retirement. We started to talk about applying to grad school. I always thought I wanted to become a social worker and dreamed of getting my master's in social work at Boston University or Boston College. During that session, Dena asked me if I ever thought about public health and pursuing a master's in that field (MPH) rather than an MSW. Before that moment, I had not thought much about public health, nor did I really know what someone with an MPH did. I liked the idea of a change of direction though, and the more I learned that public health could allow me to do what I did for "fun" (advocacy, activism, creating organizations) as a job, I started applying to grad school.

While preparing to apply for grad school, I recognized I needed to address things with Dr. T. Working with Dena helped me restore more of my voice and gave me the courage to look for a new psychiatrist who could manage my medication.

In search of someone who I felt would "hear me," I reached back out to my first therapist, Kathy. I asked Kathy about her friend, Stacy, who was a Mental Health Nurse Practitioner, a.k.a., someone who could work with me and manage my medication.

I got Stacy's email address from Kathy on a Tuesday afternoon, and by Tuesday night I had set up an appointment with Stacy for that Friday.

Stacy is different from any therapist or psychiatrist I have worked with before. She is the perfect blend of being both blunt and incredibly compassionate, making me feel safe and excited to be working with her. When I met Stacy, she was appropriately validating my OCD concerns and diagnosed me with the disorder pretty quickly. As a result, we tried new medications. Stacy always supported me in advocating for myself and listening to my body if things didn't feel right. And there were many times they didn't, but we kept trying. Like Dena and Kathy, Stacy has always believed in me and I imagine will always be cheering me on. Lucky for me, this means Dakota, Stacy's beautiful and gentle Bernese mountain dog who sits in on our sessions, will be there as well.

✓ PREHEAT THE OVEN TO 350F

✓ BEGIN TO MAKE CAKE BY ADDING:
1 CUP WATER
1/3 CUP OIL
3 EGGS

✓ MIX INGREDIENTS IN A BOWL

✓ BAKE FOR 18-20 MINUTES

✓ LET CAKE COOL.

✓ ONCE CAKE IS COOLED, CRUMBLE CAKE UNTIL IT RESEMBLES FINE CRUMBS

✓ ADD IN TWO CANS OF FROSTING TO THE BOWL OF FINE CRUMBS. ADD IN
FROSTING A LITTLE BIT AT A TIME TO ENSURE YOU STILL HAVE A LITTLE
CRUMBLE.

✓ USING AN ICE CREAM SCOOP OR SPOON, SCOOP TWO CAKE MIXTURE BALLS
WORTH OF DOUGH AND ROLL IN A TIGHT BALL.

✓ CONTINUE UNTIL ALL DOUGH IS ROLLED INTO TIGHT BALLS

✓ MELT TWO TO THREE OUNCES OF YOUR FAVORITE CHOCOLATE IN THE
MICROWAVE.

✓ DIP THE TIP OF THE CAKE POP STICKS INTO THE CHOCOLATE AND INSERT
THEM INTO THE CAKE BALLS ABOUT HALFWAY. THIS WILL SECURE THEM
THROUGH THE PROCESS

✓ FREEZE FOR 20 MINUTES

✓ MEANWHILE PREPARE DECORATING SUPPLIES

BAKER'S NOTES

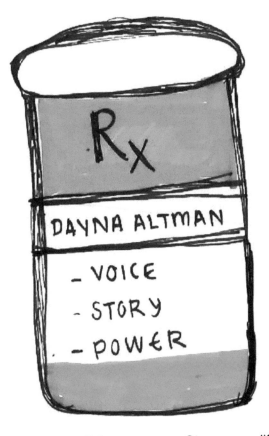

Finding my new medicine manager, Stacy, was difficult to say the least. This prescription bottle drawing is my own take on the other things that have helped me in healing.

I had this "homemade" (very homemade) flag next to my desk every year at NU. I wanted to be reminded what I was working for.

MCLEAN HOSPITAL

If you can't read my handwriting: "I had this homemade' (very) homemade flag next to my desk every year at NU. I wanted to be reminded of what I was working for."

Evening of Empowerment

INSPIRED WOMEN INSPIRE WOMEN

[Dayna Altman]

An enthusiastic and compassionate young professional, Dayna has dedicated her life to helping and empowering others. From her position as a Clinical Educator at McLean psychiatric Hospital to her personal platform projects such as "The BEA[YOU]TIFUL Project" and "Erasing Excuses," Dayna works to inspire others both in practice and through leading by example to overcome whatever obstacles one may face.

When not directly helping others, Dayna's "me" time includes writing (she is currently working on a memoir), making greeting cards(with work-in-progress calligraphy skills), Zumba and consuming two to five (depending on the difficulty of the day) cans of diet coke (there are worse "bad habits").

Inspirations include the resilience of the teens that she works with and the teachers she has had throughout her life.

As part of "The BEA(YOU)TIFUL Project", I created a series called "Evenings of Empowerment". These were hosted at various community centers where people shared their stories. From overcoming obstacles to living with mental illness, these were opportunities for people to listen to inspirational stories and come together afterwards for a larger conversation. Each person who shared got a little "bio" for promotional reasons. I read this back now and it sounds like nothing has changed.

It was very difficult to create large scale events after graduating from NU, so I used several social media platforms to share my messages. This is a photo I took for Instagram. This says "YOU ARE MORE THAN THIS" (on a scale)in honor of National Eating Disorders Awareness Month in February.

When I was applying to grad school, I decided to get glasses. I have always had terrible eyesight but had ignored it up until this point. I didn't want to not do well on the GRE because I couldn't read the questions! So I went to the eye doctor and this is the day I got my glasses; I remember because I went to my favorite local ice cream spot after with my dad. Now I can't imagine my life without my glasses, both in terms of associating them with my personality and because I love being able to see!

MELT THE REMAINING CHOCOLATE IN A BOWL. MAKE SURE
YOU HAVE ENOUGH TO SUBMERGE THE ENTIRE CAKE BALL.

As I waited for decision letters from graduate schools, I continued
to look for outlets to manage my mental health. A new colleague
began at McLean, and she told me about SoulCycle; I was in-
trigued. I had only heard of SoulCycle through the Netflix show
Unbreakable Kimmy Schmidt, but I wanted to give it a try.

I cannot think of a better metaphor for SoulCycle in the context of
this recipe than "melt the..." and not just because of the way I
sweat in SoulCycle but because when I went (and still, when I go),
everything I felt outside of the room melted away. I found peace
and refuge in the sport. I learned how to better manage my anxiety in the moment both on and off the bike. SoulCycle is about
community and building a "pack." Every instructor encourages
their riders to show up for their team (or the others in the class),
and I found not only an extension of my heart in SoulCycle, I
found friends, specifically my favorite instructor, Liah.

Liah is just incredibly cool, and I love her because she thinks
kindness, hard work and authenticity are just as cool. Both her
classes and Liah herself helped me overcome so much, including
the 2016 election. She encouraged everyone to let what was
happening outside of the four walls of the SoulCycle studio be
outside, even if it was just for forty-five minutes. I opened up to
Liah about surviving a sexual assault in a way that I had not
opened up to anyone. With Liah, there was no judgement. Expec-
tations melted away, and only love was front and center.

—-

My life became about both work and SoulCyle. Out of seemingly
nowhere one day though, I sat in the chart (staff) room at work
finishing up notes. My phone beeped with an email that had the
subject line: "Congratulations from Active Minds!!!" As much as
Active Minds, the mental health organization for college students,
was a part of my college experience, I wasn't involved with it for
too long after college. I read on to learn that I had been nominat-
ed for an award by the co-founder of the NU chapter at their annual conference, and I won "Distinguished Alumni of the Year". I

was incredibly excited, but it was in Sacramento, California. I didn't quite know how I would get there, so I put it out to my community, and I was completely submerged in love and celebration. I raised money through a GoFundMe page and a private donor to touch down in Sacramento the day before I would receive my award.

Activism and mental health advocacy had been important to me since the moment I was diagnosed with anxiety, depression and an eating disorder at PC. The experience in Sacramento was so special; not only did I receive the most beautiful award, also I was continuously inspired by the people I met there who were also working hard to change the conversation around mental health. These inspirations, specifically Cassandra and Allison, became good friends, and friends I still keep in touch with to this day. I was also proud of myself for taking on a travel excursion alone. Ever since traveling to Israel, getting on a plane, especially alone, has been scary. Every time I do it, it gets easier though, and my wounds heal a little more.

As much as my truth was utter inspiration during that trip, I do remember being significantly concerned about my weight. I was convinced I was gaining weight each day that passed, but getting some distance from that trip, I realized that I was at the lowest weight I have ever been through my eating disorder journey. I think I was very much projecting my fear about my mom onto myself. My mom had been obsessed with her weight and submerged in her own eating disorder since before I was born, but this was the first time it was externally visible to the world. She was wasting away as a skeleton of a person, and I was so scared. I began to become angry with her often out of total fear and defense. I recognized, even on a subconscious level, being upset with her was easier than being so scared for her and the threat she posed to her life every time she chose her eating disorder.

By the end of the year, I recognized I had accomplished a lot in 2016. Working and being promoted at McLean, discovering SoulCycle, my trip to Sacramento and getting into graduate school. I was proud to have a few options when it came to making the decision to pursue my MPH. And, although I originally did not know much about NU's Master of Public Health program, I did know a lot about NU and how much it felt like home. I weighed my options, and the Double Husky scholarship certainly didn't hurt. I accepted the offer and went earlier than I had expected; I was going to start in January 2017 rather than the following fall. I was excited to be embarking on a new chapter, and even more excited that I would get to do this at "home."

✓ PREHEAT THE OVEN TO 350F

✓ BEGIN TO MAKE CAKE BY ADDING:
1 CUP WATER
1/3 CUP OIL
3 EGGS

✓ MIX INGREDIENTS IN A BOWL

✓ BAKE FOR 18-20 MINUTES

✓ LET CAKE COOL.

✓ ONCE CAKE IS COOLED, CRUMBLE CAKE UNTIL IT RESEMBLES FINE CRUMBS

✓ ADD IN TWO CANS OF FROSTING TO THE BOWL OF FINE CRUMBS. ADD IN
FROSTING A LITTLE BIT AT A TIME TO ENSURE YOU STILL HAVE A LITTLE
CRUMBLE.

✓ USING AN ICE CREAM SCOOP OR SPOON, SCOOP TWO CAKE MIXTURE BALLS
WORTH OF DOUGH AND ROLL IN A TIGHT BALL.

✓ CONTINUE UNTIL ALL DOUGH IS ROLLED INTO TIGHT BALLS

✓ MELT TWO TO THREE OUNCES OF YOUR FAVORITE CHOCOLATE IN THE
MICROWAVE.

✓ DIP THE TIP OF THE CAKE POP STICKS INTO THE CHOCOLATE AND INSERT
THEM INTO THE CAKE BALLS ABOUT HALFWAY. THIS WILL SECURE THEM
THROUGH THE PROCESS

✓ FREEZE FOR 20 MINUTES

✓ MEANWHILE PREPARE DECORATING SUPPLIES

✓ MELT THE REMAINING CHOCOLATE IN A BOWL. MAKE SURE YOU HAVE ENOUGH
TO SUBMERGE THE ENTIRE CAKE BALL.

BAKER'S NOTES

This is the moment that I won my award on be-half of Active Minds. Here I am (worried I was going to fall over on stage in my shoes) with Founder, Alison Malmon. Alison continues to be a mental health advocacy role model for me!

When I came back from the Active Minds Conference, I was asked to speak at my alma mater, Algonquin Regional High School! Two of my favorite teachers asked if I would come share my mental health story with their classes. I remember when I drove in and I saw this sign, I couldn't stop smiling, I had to get out and take a selfie! I am proud to say, sharing my story at Algonquin is now a bi-yearly occurrence!

Once I started riding at SoulCycle, I was all in!
Instructors at SoulCycle often host theme rides
where they get dressed up as the artist they are
featuring! When Liah decided to do a Sia theme
ride, I was ready to dress up with her! Not just
because I love Sia but because I wanted Liah to
know she never had to do "it" (anything) alone!

HAPPY BIRTHDAY! ♡PORT

Birthdays at SoulCycle are such special birthdays! I am so grateful to have spent every birthday since discovering SoulCycle on the bike! This is from my first SoulCycle birthday and it is still my favorite polaroid.

This is a photo from my last day working at McLean Hospital in late December 2016. I remember someone said it was like a "holiday." I still smile when I think of that.

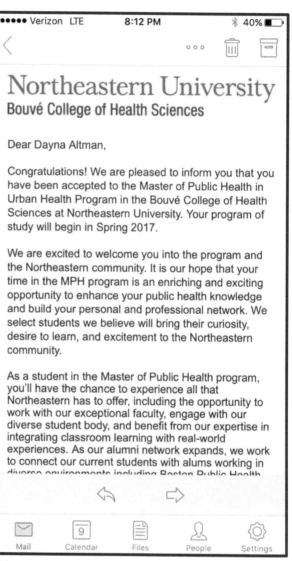

Northeastern University
Bouvé College of Health Sciences

Dear Dayna Altman,

Congratulations! We are pleased to inform you that you have been accepted to the Master of Public Health in Urban Health Program in the Bouvé College of Health Sciences at Northeastern University. Your program of study will begin in Spring 2017.

We are excited to welcome you into the program and the Northeastern community. It is our hope that your time in the MPH program is an enriching and exciting opportunity to enhance your public health knowledge and build your personal and professional network. We select students we believe will bring their curiosity, desire to learn, and excitement to the Northeastern community.

As a student in the Master of Public Health program, you'll have the chance to experience all that Northeastern has to offer, including the opportunity to work with our exceptional faculty, engage with our diverse student body, and benefit from our expertise in integrating classroom learning with real-world experiences. As our alumni network expands, we work to connect our current students with alums working in diverse environments including Boston Public Health

My acceptance letter into the MPH Program at Northeastern University!

REMOVE CAKE BALLS FROM FREEZER

Going back to NU for graduate school at first brought a sense of comfort. That time that I wished I could freeze? It started to become a dream come true. I got to see my mentee turned best friend Julia all the time, and I had moved closer to J, as I was back on campus and we were going on about three years of our relationship. However, going back to school brought up some old negative coping skills too, including using grades to identify my worth. I had worked so hard to detach from this old coping mechanism, but there was something about seeing a number on a test and automatically feeling I was that number that was harder than I thought to break.

I was also scared because Dena was going on her second maternity leave. My mind and heart were filled with thoughts of fear and sadness yet again. She asked if it would help to know that it was another boy. I sighed with relief and nodded. She said, "Yeah, it's funny how that worked out."

My time was filled with evening classes and a graduate assistantship at NU. A few weeks before I began my classes, I was offered a graduate assistantship at an office on campus. This was in large part landed as a result of the positive relationships and legacy I built at NU as an undergraduate student. I was especially excited to start this new job, as it allowed me to professionally work in sexual violence prevention.

This coincided with my first time opening up publicly on social media, to my friends and extended family, about being sexually assaulted. Up until this point, I worked hard as an advocate but I never shared my own experience. On the third anniversary of the assault, I decided I would share. I worked with a local dance company to perform a lyrical piece exploring my survivorship. The company choreographed the dance but I chose the song: "Bird Set Free" by Sia. I first heard the song in SoulCycle a few months prior, and I felt so emotionally connected to the lyrics. When I decided to pursue coming forward about being assaulted in the form of a dance, I knew this was the song I would choose.

After a few sessions with the choreographers, they suggested that I expand this dance beyond a solo piece. They told me their senior dancers on their elite team would be a great addition. I worked with the senior girls tirelessly to put our best feet forward (quite literally). I also felt working with the girls was a unique opportunity for me to model vulnerability and honesty to them. I felt I showed the importance of "owning your story, not your shame."

Working on performing and filming this dance truly helped me "take out" and revisit what I was feeling, and the shame I had built up in my brain and body over the years. On New Year's Day, I released the video, and was met with overwhelming support. The video even got attention from BuzzFeed; once again, I felt I was making that impact I had always wanted.

A few days later after coming off the "high" of the video release, I began working in the assistantship role. Working day in and day out on prevention initiatives was so exciting. This position also allowed me to be heavily involved in planning NU's first Take Back the Night (TBTN) event. TBTN is a national initiative that takes place during April for Sexual Assault Awareness Month. I had attended TBNT at PC years before I was assaulted, and it left me speechless. Typically, stories are shared and sometimes music is played. While there are tears and grief, there is typically a message of hope just by seeing the support of so many community members listening to and seeing survivors. When the topic of choosing speakers for NU's first TBTN came up, I volunteered and was supported tremendously by the graduate assistantship team. I practiced my speech for all the staff members and my friends. I quickly recognized my own gaps and limitations in my healing, specifically around not feeling my story was "good enough," or "bad enough," rather. I constantly feared my story was inferior or boring. As hard as it was to feel this rush of shame and insecurity during our dress rehearsal, it became a message I wanted to share. Just like my first therapist, Kathy, always said, "There is no comparison of misery," and I truly learned to lean into this piece of me. I realized if I was worried that my story was inferior, so many others probably do too. I wanted to model vulnerability for them—for all of the people who felt silenced by their own shame.

The night of TBNT, I was shaking with nerves. I was up first to speak, but the minute I squeezed the hand of my designated "support person," I got up there and I told my story—no shame, no hesitation. I was funny at times and charming, but not in the way I had felt I needed to be all along, rather in a way that felt authentic to my story. When I finished, I got a standing ovation and a chill rushed down my spine; it was once again confirmed: This is exactly where I needed to be.

The rest of the semester was filled with a similar type of hunger for advocacy. I created a third organization called "Changing the Tape" that hosted community events promoting acceptance of anxiety and OCD. I once again attended Mariska's Hargitay's Joyful Heart Foundation (JHF) gala in 2017 to support survivors of sexual assault and domestic violence. After the gala, I was offered the opportunity to join the JHF staff at the premiere of *I Am Evidence*. *I Am Evidence* is a film Mariska Hargitay created about the rape kit backlog in the US. Like Mariska felt initially moved by the stories of survivors she was hearing when she started JHF, as she became more involved in advocating for survivors, she began to learn about the rape kit backlog. *I Am Evidence* told the stories of several survivors whose lives were turned upside down as a result of both being assaulted and the years of waiting for their rape kits to be tested. In one of the cases as a result of the backlog, several assaults with a serial perpetrator occurred. It was so moving to hear from each of the survivors, knowing if the rape kits had been tested, there could have arguably been many women saved from trauma. I sat in that crowded movie theater during the Tribeca Film Festival in mid-April, literally stunned. The film itself was powerful, but so is everything Mariska does. What struck me outside the film itself was the "talk back" afterwards. Mariska and several of the women in the film facilitated a discussion with the audience. I saw the way people took a tangible form of advocacy and the conversation it built, the call to action it inspired, and I wanted that, I needed that in my next project. So, in Dayna fashion, I didn't wait a moment to spring into action.

After the screening, I met my mom at Domino's Pizza, where she had been visiting an old friend while I was in the theater. We got in the car and I grabbed a pen. On the cardboard pizza box, I began creating an outline for my first documentary project. Although I didn't know the structure or the format yet, I knew it would show-case healing modalities of survivors and portray the non-linear process it entails. I wasn't sure how yet, but I knew I was going to do it.

- ✓ PREHEAT THE OVEN TO 350F

- ✓ BEGIN TO MAKE CAKE BY ADDING:
  1 CUP WATER
  1/3 CUP OIL
  3 EGGS

- ✓ MIX INGREDIENTS IN A BOWL

- ✓ BAKE FOR 18-20 MINUTES

- ✓ LET CAKE COOL.

- ✓ ONCE CAKE IS COOLED, CRUMBLE CAKE UNTIL IT RESEMBLES FINE CRUMBS

- ✓ ADD IN TWO CANS OF FROSTING TO THE BOWL OF FINE CRUMBS. ADD IN FROSTING A LITTLE BIT AT A TIME TO ENSURE YOU STILL HAVE A LITTLE CRUMBLE.

- ✓ USING AN ICE CREAM SCOOP OR SPOON, SCOOP TWO CAKE MIXTURE BALLS WORTH OF DOUGH AND ROLL IN A TIGHT BALL.

- ✓ CONTINUE UNTIL ALL DOUGH IS ROLLED INTO TIGHT BALLS

- ✓ MELT TWO TO THREE OUNCES OF YOUR FAVORITE CHOCOLATE IN THE MICROWAVE.

- ✓ DIP THE TIP OF THE CAKE POP STICKS INTO THE CHOCOLATE AND INSERT THEM INTO THE CAKE BALLS ABOUT HALFWAY. THIS WILL SECURE THEM THROUGH THE PROCESS

- ✓ FREEZE FOR 20 MINUTES

- ✓ MEANWHILE PREPARE DECORATING SUPPLIES

- ✓ MELT THE REMAINING CHOCOLATE IN A BOWL. MAKE SURE YOU HAVE ENOUGH TO SUBMERGE THE ENTIRE CAKE BALL.

- ✓ REMOVE CAKE BALLS FROM FREEZER

BAKER'S NOTES

This is a group photo from the dance music video that I released on January 1, 2017. I am so glad I performed this piece with these girls and I loved that we incorporated paint with the message we sent. *"And I don't care if I sing off key, I find myself in my melodies. I sing for love, I sing for me, I shout it out like a bird set free"* - Sia

I continued the "Evenings of Empowerment" during the winter of 2017. I was so happy to bring back these nights of storytelling and community in the Boston area with some wonderful friends. From (left): Me, Carly, Julia, Catherine, Nick and Martha.

Here I am telling my story at the First Annual "Take Back the Night" at Northeastern University, April 2017. Getting a standing ovation that night sent the most incredible chill down my spine.

The Joyful Heart Foundation Gala in 2017, NYC. Truly, the most beautiful dress I think I will ever own---if I can somehow wear this on my wedding day I will.

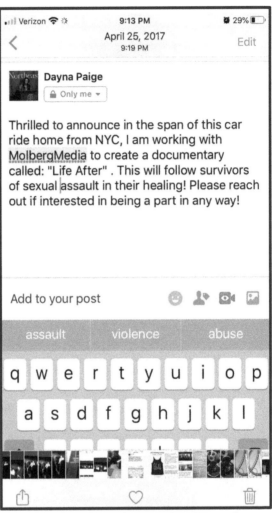

April 25, 2017
9:19 PM

Edit

Dayna Paige
🔒 Only me ▾

Thrilled to announce in the span of this car ride home from NYC, I am working with MolbergMedia to create a documentary called: "Life After" . This will follow survivors of sexual assault in their healing! Please reach out if interested in being a part in any way!

Add to your post

assault   violence   abuse

9:13PM: It only took me a few hours to launch into planning mode on that night. Note, I loved working with Molberg Media for the dance music video and was excited to do so again (as I posted)! Unfortunately, we didn't get to work together due to distance and scheduling conflicts but Molberg Media came up with the name for the documentary!

DIP CAKE BALLS CAREFULLY INTO THE CHOCOLATE UNTIL COVERED.

I quickly dipped into my network to find a filmmaker, and almost immediately Liam was recommended to me. Liam was a film student who was very active in the Northeastern film club NUTV. He took on the project for experience, and I paid him back in endless pizza and burritos during the filming process.

While I originally wanted to tell several stories of survivors, I wanted to start with my own. I knew I wanted to cover several identities and stories but I believed I was a great place to start. So, Liam and I filmed almost three times a week for about a month. We were on a tight timeline, as we were racing against the end of the spring semester and summer schedule before Liam would leave Boston for a co-op.

We got very creative! We filmed me speaking, incorporated my music video and even went to film at a local mikveh. A mikveh is a place with a natural source of water which facilitates several Jewish rituals. Originally used for religious women after their menstrual cycle or to facilitate the process of those who decided to convert to Judaism, a mikveh is a historical and religious practice. Mikveh has been reclaimed though by several trauma survivors as a symbol of healing. I experienced a mikveh for the film. While each experience was special, I was most excited to film at SoulCycle, specifically in Liah's class.

Liah was one of the people who helped me feel most comfortable in embarking on this documentary, and SoulCycle is a place of total empowerment for me. Before we got started, Liah explained why there was a camera in the front of the studio and the purpose of the film. I remember when the first song played and we began jogging to the beat, Liah yelled "Yeah, Dayna!" and the community cheered after hearing my name. I felt completely "covered" in love.

—

Once the filming was complete, we began the editing process and putting the story together, splicing in interviews with experts.

I began planning the premiere in August and leaned into telling my complete story in a new and tangible way.

Once we wrapped the documentary, the summer continued and I fell into a slight depression. Like with grades, I was in a place where projects helped me evaluate my worth, so much so that my treatment team—Dena and my medicine manager, Stacy—had me try to take a "break" from passion projects in hopes of separating my worth from productivity; this was so hard. Additionally, I had little structure since my graduate assistantship placement was not able to fund my position for the summer, so I was generally stuck within the confines of my own mind.

—

About a month later, on the way to a Friday morning SoulCycle class, I got into the (remember the preface so long ago?!) serious car accident. I was making a left turn out of my neighborhood, and while I was turning, I was hit full speed in the passenger window and door. The airbags deployed, and I remember waiting to wake up from this nightmare. I called my parents and they came racing down to the edge of our neighborhood. I hysterically cried when the ambulance arrived checking out my collarbone and burn from the seatbelt. There was little damage to the other car, but mine was totaled. I was already trying to manage this depressive episode, and quite literally hitting a new rock bottom was painful. I saw Kathy occasionally and Dena consistently working through this sadness and emptiness. I also began to feel a distance between myself and J. We had become very comfortable in our routine, and I felt there was a lack of mutual effort, which was so hard to admit. I also recognized that I was scared to be totally honest with him about where I was mentally, which spoke a lot about the relationship itself.

✓ PREHEAT THE OVEN TO 350F

✓ BEGIN TO MAKE CAKE BY ADDING:
  1 CUP WATER
  1/3 CUP OIL
  3 EGGS

✓ MIX INGREDIENTS IN A BOWL

✓ BAKE FOR 18-20 MINUTES

✓ LET CAKE COOL.

✓ ONCE CAKE IS COOLED, CRUMBLE CAKE UNTIL IT RESEMBLES FINE CRUMBS

✓ ADD IN TWO CANS OF FROSTING TO THE BOWL OF FINE CRUMBS. ADD IN
  FROSTING A LITTLE BIT AT A TIME TO ENSURE YOU STILL HAVE A LITTLE
  CRUMBLE.

✓ USING AN ICE CREAM SCOOP OR SPOON, SCOOP TWO CAKE MIXTURE BALLS
  WORTH OF DOUGH AND ROLL IN A TIGHT BALL.

✓ CONTINUE UNTIL ALL DOUGH IS ROLLED INTO TIGHT BALLS

✓ MELT TWO TO THREE OUNCES OF YOUR FAVORITE CHOCOLATE IN THE
  MICROWAVE.

✓ DIP THE TIP OF THE CAKE POP STICKS INTO THE CHOCOLATE AND INSERT
  THEM INTO THE CAKE BALLS ABOUT HALFWAY. THIS WILL SECURE THEM
  THROUGH THE PROCESS

✓ FREEZE FOR 20 MINUTES

✓ MEANWHILE PREPARE DECORATING SUPPLIES

✓ MELT THE REMAINING CHOCOLATE IN A BOWL. MAKE SURE YOU HAVE ENOUGH
  TO SUBMERGE THE ENTIRE CAKE BALL.

✓ REMOVE CAKE BALLS FROM FREEZER

✓ DIP CAKE BALLS CAREFULLY INTO THE CHOCOLATE UNTIL COVERED.

BAKER'S NOTES

This was the second day of filming for *Life After: The Film.* I wanted to make sure I portrayed how healing sharing my story can be! Liam is behind the camera here.

Everything you do, everything you work on, everything you are is absolutely amazing

I'm taking a screenshot lol

I remember after we wrapped the filming of *Life After,* I was really doubting my own worth outside of the project. Happy to still have this screenshot from my friend, Jenna, reminding me, it's not just what I work on, it's who I am.

This was taken on my cousin's trampoline at a family re-union a few days after my car accident. I remember this moment so vividly. I was really hurting but on the outside, I was nailing my split on the trampoline....outwardly present and smiling with my family. Appearing "happy" or "perfect" or "smiling" all the time was one of my biggest barriers to getting the help I needed. No one knew how much I was hurting. This is something I am still working on. Authentically speaking my truth but also authentically "looking" my truth.

LET THE EXCESS CHOCOLATE DRIP OFF. SHAKE OR SWIRL IF NECESSARY

On August 27, 2017, exactly one week after my twenty-fifth birthday, I premiered *Life After: The Film*. There were appetizers and centerpieces, and the director of the NU MPH program led a meaningful discussion after the audience screened the film. I got up in front of the crowd to thank everyone for coming, and everyone stood. I felt an overwhelming sense of pride. I let everything else going on outside of that summer drip away. I let a toxic friendship go; I let go of the shame I carried since my experience in Israel in 2013. I recognized that in that moment, my people saw me, and it felt good to be seen.

I was so grateful to be surrounded by so many people I loved that night, including a new close friend, Brenna. During the mutually difficult summer of 2017, Brenna and I supported one another. She saw me and my love for advocacy, and I saw her and her love for photography. She not only took the photos at the premiere, but she also was the first person to support and collaborate with me on my mental health cookbook.

The "break" from projects did not last long, and I dove into combining my new passion for baking with mental health storytelling. I started off by interviewing people and collecting narratives along with their favorite recipes. Early on in the process, Brenna and I cleared off my kitchen counter and we took photos for the cover. I dreamed about what it would be like to see myself on the shelves of Barnes & Noble.

While creating the cookbook, I began to see a shift in my body. This started with SoulCycle; I became more muscular with every class, but I was also gaining weight. In some ways this was necessary, in some ways not. It became a point of tension in my relationship with J, and he encouraged me to diet. I thought back to the beginning of our relationship and how he recognized that my eating disorder had truly taken so much away from me, and now he was encouraging it. He began to say additional things that broke my heart, including the proclamation that just my existence was affecting his mental health, and we made the difficult decision to take a break.

151

This break paralleled with a forced leave of absence from my graduate assistantship. I brought the flood of emotions that consumed me about J into work each day. In many moments, I think about the way I carried myself at my assistantship, and I cringe. It has been hard to find compassion for myself at that time, as so much shame continues to cloud that experience. When I was asked to take a break from the assistantship, I was assured it was just a break. It was a break out of love and compassion. The team knew I would not take a voluntary leave, so they thought it was best for me if that were not an option. My life was swirling out of control, and I was losing my sense of structure. I was hurting so much that Dena and I discussed going back to treatment, specifically at the Renfrew Center, a program in downtown Boston, while I was on leave. This was a day program for those who were struggling with eating disorders and the related disorders that usually accompany EDs: anxiety, depression, trauma. I was really angry to be there at first and was surprisingly resistant. I remember every other day when they took "weights" they asked the patients to look at the number on the scale. This was a different approach than the other treatment I received and it was terrifying.

I remember when I first saw the number, I broke down. I thought about what my eating disordered eighteen-year-old self would think about this number, and I hated myself. Once I began to see the benefit of being in the program though, I was able to process and begin to accept living in this new body. I also began to open up to my favorite clinician, Angela, about the trauma I had endured in my life through a "trauma group" she ran. I wrote a detailed narrative of my experiences and shared it with the group. This was not just about the trauma I endured in Israel but about the way I was being treated during the end of my first serious relationship.

J will always be my first love and it was painful to let him go, but it was undoubtedly the best decision for us. As hard as it was to let the excess self-hatred drift away, I relied on my "team": my treatment team, but also my friends during this unknown period. My support system continued to be important when I learned a few hours after the official breakup with J that I would not be invited back to the graduate assistantship.

I had been at Renfrew for about two weeks and had emailed both my direct boss and the overall supervisor that I was ready to come back. They asked for a phone call, which instinctively felt bad. I held in my tears when they told me they would collect the things from my desk and mail them to me. It wasn't just about being fired; it felt personal. I thought back to how special I felt during TBTN, how valued and important I saw myself in the context of that job. I was confused through this whole process, as they said one thing and delivered another. Before I left I was asked to send them updates on how I was doing via email. I felt especially crushed when I got an email back from my supervisor while standing in line at B.Good after my first week at Renfrew. She asked me why I was emailing her and to identify other supports. I felt gaslit and confused, having been promised one thing to my face and then getting something different each time.

If this was not hurtful enough, a few days later a classmate forwarded me a job description for my position, outlining exactly what they did not want—essentially all characteristics that I brought to the job. If my classmate was able to identify me for the posting, I could just imagine who else could. The lawyer in my mom encouraged me to think about suing for character defamation, but I didn't think that's what I wanted. I didn't want revenge... I was grieving and I was embarrassed. While I take full responsibility for my part in the end, I also have come to feel justified in my anger for the way it was handled.

—

A very real and humiliating piece of being let go was having to rely on my parents for money. Excess material things began to go while I was searching for a new job and also trying to manage my fall classes. The cookbook became a beacon of light in my life, as I continued to work on collecting stories and creating mental health resource pages to intersperse in the book.

Along with progress in the book, I finally found a part-time job I was excited about. In January 2018, I started co-running the dining room in a homeless shelter on the weekends. My "co-pilot" was a woman named Tanaysha. The two of us were responsible for the dining room and its operations in all ways. We trained volunteer groups, greeted the guests and broke up fights; there were a lot of those. Tanaysha and I approached our work so differently, and at first it seemed unimaginable to learn from one another. As time passed though, we learned to work together in a way I could not have fathomed the first time I met her. We found our own roles, and we ultimately became close, which I certainly needed after my first date on Hinge, another dating app, in February of 2018.

My first Hinge date led to a short but traumatic experience. We got way too serious way too fast until I slept over one night and woke up to him assaulting me in my sleep. At first I didn't know if this counted as assault. And then I thought about all of the work I did for survivors and how educated I became on the topic, including if you cannot give consent, you do not have consent. I thought about sticking it out, out of pure fear, and then I remembered on our second date he showed me where he kept his gun. This was a scary road to go down and I am very grateful for Dena for encouraging me to get out as fast I could, and I am lucky that I did.

I wasn't sure how to handle this one. It brought new challenges, including being tested for STIs. As scary as it was to even be living this nightmare, I would have never met Kendra at NU Health Services Center without this experience.

Kendra made me feel so safe after truly one of the worst experiences I had. She made sure I had academic resources and support. She called and checked in on me at least once a week. She cared in a way I never saw a physician do. We truly bonded, and I will never forget the role she played in this time. In fact, I saw how different things were when I was supported and believed immediately. My healing involved less shame, and I felt comfortable discussing what I had been through. I even awarded Kendra with an outstanding provider award while I was completing my practicum for my MPH that semester at Beth Israel Deaconess Medical Center.

✓ PREHEAT THE OVEN TO 350F

✓ BEGIN TO MAKE CAKE BY ADDING:
1 CUP WATER
1/3 CUP OIL
3 EGGS

✓ MIX INGREDIENTS IN A BOWL

✓ BAKE FOR 18-20 MINUTES

✓ LET CAKE COOL.

✓ ONCE CAKE IS COOLED, CRUMBLE CAKE UNTIL IT RESEMBLES FINE CRUMBS

✓ ADD IN TWO CANS OF FROSTING TO THE BOWL OF FINE CRUMBS. ADD IN
FROSTING A LITTLE BIT AT A TIME TO ENSURE YOU STILL HAVE A LITTLE
CRUMBLE.

✓ USING AN ICE CREAM SCOOP OR SPOON, SCOOP TWO CAKE MIXTURE BALLS
WORTH OF DOUGH AND ROLL IN A TIGHT BALL.

✓ CONTINUE UNTIL ALL DOUGH IS ROLLED INTO TIGHT BALLS

✓ MELT TWO TO THREE OUNCES OF YOUR FAVORITE CHOCOLATE IN THE
MICROWAVE.

✓ DIP THE TIP OF THE CAKE POP STICKS INTO THE CHOCOLATE AND INSERT
THEM INTO THE CAKE BALLS ABOUT HALFWAY. THIS WILL SECURE THEM
THROUGH THE PROCESS

✓ FREEZE FOR 20 MINUTES

✓ MEANWHILE PREPARE DECORATING SUPPLIES

✓ MELT THE REMAINING CHOCOLATE IN A BOWL. MAKE SURE YOU HAVE ENOUGH
TO SUBMERGE THE ENTIRE CAKE BALL.

✓ REMOVE CAKE BALLS FROM FREEZER

✓ DIP CAKE BALLS CAREFULLY INTO THE CHOCOLATE UNTIL COVERED.

✓ LET THE EXCESS CHOCOLATE DRIP OFF. SHAKE OR SWIRL IF NECESSARY

BAKER'S NOTES

As much as the Summer of 2017 brought me: being Brenna's friend was one of the best gifts I received and one I continue to cherish. She took the photos the night of the *Life After: The Film* premiere and now I don't go to anyone else when I am in need of pictures. I am so proud to be her friend in all ways!

The night of the *Life After: The Film* premiere with Julia and Nick! These two were truly my rocks through this process. They were on my " event board" and helped me plan the premiere! Julia has truly been with me through it all, I treasure our friendship and all of the memories from "Fashion in Action" to *Life After* and beyond.

My parents and I at my premiere.

I was able to host the premiere at the NU Alumni Center: a gorgeous space on campus that brought together so many people I love. One of the most memorable and best nights to date.

SoulCycle continued to be an outlet amidst all of the change and chaos in the fall of 2017. It was nice to still have a place to celebrate my strength and my friends in the studio. From left: Liah, me, Steph and Allie.

After my time at the Renfrew Center, Brenna and I did an impromptu photoshoot at one of our favorite spots near Southboro: Hopkinton State Park. We were not planning on taking photos that day, just a walk but Brenna encouraged me to own everything I had been through during this pop-up photoshoot. I am so glad she did because this is one of my favorite photos she has taken of me. And because she is right! As much as I tell others to own their stories, I needed to do the same.

Through it all, I continued to pursue my public speaking "career" and received these cards after one of my bi-annual trips to my high school. I save all of the cards in a box under my bed and look back at them when I need to.

In addition to speaking, I began to show my documentary at colleges and universities across the country! This is a photo from a screening at Quinnipiac University in Connecticut.

ADD THE SPRINKLES WHILE THE CHOCOLATE IS STILL WET.

Even though I was worried about jumping back into dating, while my wounds were still very much open, A came along. Well, he was always there... sitting in the back of my Thursday night human sexuality class, but one night during our fifteen-minute break in late March we struck up a conversation at the water fountain. I really liked how I connected with A immediately, and we started dating pretty quickly after our serendipitous water fountain moment.

I was still healing in many ways from Hinge, from J, from Israel... but I got to do this along with A. I loved that he supported me during my events and often "sold" some of my ideas better than (or just as well as) I did, and I felt genuinely happy. We grew together during this time. We both walked across the graduation stage, earning our respective master's degrees and in support of one another. Little did I know I would rely on A just a few days later when my mom was rushed to the emergency room.

My mom had not felt well for a long time, and she felt it was related to her Crohn's Disease. She was getting blood tests and nothing was helping. Her symptoms were getting worse when she came back from a trip to New Orleans with my dad. My mom called an on-call doctor about her bleeding and the doctor encouraged her to go to the ER immediately in case it was related to the flight she had just taken.

When my mom entered the hospital, she went directly from the ER to the ICU. My dad was leaving for California the next day for work, and he asked the doctor if he felt she would be discharged or if he should cancel his trip. The attending doctor felt she would be discharged in the morning, so my dad got on a plane to California the next day.

While my dad flew to California, I was in my second day of a summer job working as a SAFEPLAN advocate in a local court. SAFEPLAN is a court-based program that funds and supports advocacy services for those who are filing restraining or harassment orders in a court. The restraining order process is extremely difficult and is complicated by legal jargon, so SAFEPLAN advo-

164

cates become comfortable with the process to explain its different elements to those who need them. I was on my second day of the job when I left early to visit my mom in the hospital. She had wanted me to wait until after the work day, but I could not focus. I remember when I walked into her hospital room and she tried to reassure me she was okay. She pointed at the whiteboard across from her bed saying, "Look I am okay, I am on the orange team, everyone is here to take care of me." I wanted to believe her, and the comfort she was offering in that moment was everything I wanted when I was a little girl. And here I was fifteen years later, being offered that comfort, and it was still hard to believe she was going to be okay.

Unlike what the original doctor had predicted, my mom was not going anywhere. She was transferred to a bed on the second floor of the hospital and was there for a week. As much as I was that scared eight-year-old girl inside, in that hospital room, I was the adult. I was making decisions, including one that was difficult but life changing: about a blood transfusion. To this day, I am an advocate for blood donation, as I saw the way it helped my mom. She had an emergency colonoscopy and they called it a bad flare up, which it was, but not just her Crohn's Disease. It was very hard for me to stand up and tell each doctor that came in and out of the room that there was something else going on: her eating disorder. I tried to speak and my mom would roll her eyes and say, "I am fine, Dayna. I eat, I eat all the time." I am not sure if it was my mom's defense or lack of information, but none of the doctors did much when I told them about her eating disorder.

When she left the hospital, I had a sprinkle of hope instilled back in my heart. I thought this could be enough to scare her into recovery. It lasted for a little while, and I would tell A I was encouraged, but ED (her eating disorder) always came back into her life and became the most important thing in the room. It didn't help that my dad could also not get through to her, whether it was her own stubbornness or his own denial.

After being in the hospital, my mom officially retired from her job as a lawyer and became a full-time Hot Yoga, Hot Pilates, Zumba instructor. I was happy for her but I was also scared, all the time. I worried when she made the transition and, honestly, I still worry that constant exercise is too much for her, but she loves it more than anything and I also realize this is not something I can control as much as I would like to. I learned to really embody these principles from going to Al-Anon meetings. Al-Anon is a support group for those who have a loved one with an addiction. While everyone else in the meetings had loved ones struggling with alcohol or drugs, I became well-immersed in the teachings. I remember every time I shared why I was there, I apologized, saying I know my family member doesn't struggle with drugs or alcohol but is addicted to eating disorder behaviors, and every time I was met with open arms and support. They were so welcoming and wanted me to learn from them; they invited me to meetings and gave me their phone numbers. Al-Anon is a free and wonderful resource, one that I expect to return to in the future.

As I began to find more of my voice, I poured bits of hope and energy back into the mental health cookbook. I had a vision for the book, *Bake it Till You Make it,* now more than ever. I wanted mental health to be accessible to everyone, and I saw using food as a means for storytelling and conversation as a way to do that. As I continued to build this "empire" in my head, there was a breakdown and breakup in my love life. This was tough; I truly thought I would marry A, but the love was not mutual. In fact, he told me he did not love me at a wedding. I was beside myself because I loved him so much. I couldn't figure out what was wrong with me and why this was one-sided. I came to the conclusion that I just needed to "love less." After that wedding things went downhill, and as much as I look back at A positively, there was a very real side to our relationship that was not compatible: the one where he drank. I remember driving him home once after a night out and pulling over on the side of the Mass Pike so he could throw up. He got out and grabbed the window, and I looked away. I thought to myself, "This is literally my worst nightmare, how did I get here? How did I abandon my core self this much?"

But it was because I loved him.

The relationship ended a few weeks later.

✓ PREHEAT THE OVEN TO 350F

✓ BEGIN TO MAKE CAKE BY ADDING:
1 CUP WATER
1/3 CUP OIL
3 EGGS

✓ MIX INGREDIENTS IN A BOWL

✓ BAKE FOR 18-20 MINUTES

✓ LET CAKE COOL.

✓ ONCE CAKE IS COOLED, CRUMBLE CAKE UNTIL IT RESEMBLES FINE CRUMBS

✓ ADD IN TWO CANS OF FROSTING TO THE BOWL OF FINE CRUMBS. ADD IN
FROSTING A LITTLE BIT AT A TIME TO ENSURE YOU STILL HAVE A LITTLE
CRUMBLE.

✓ USING AN ICE CREAM SCOOP OR SPOON, SCOOP TWO CAKE MIXTURE BALLS
WORTH OF DOUGH AND ROLL IN A TIGHT BALL.

✓ CONTINUE UNTIL ALL DOUGH IS ROLLED INTO TIGHT BALLS

✓ MELT TWO TO THREE OUNCES OF YOUR FAVORITE CHOCOLATE IN THE
MICROWAVE.

✓ DIP THE TIP OF THE CAKE POP STICKS INTO THE CHOCOLATE AND INSERT
THEM INTO THE CAKE BALLS ABOUT HALFWAY. THIS WILL SECURE THEM
THROUGH THE PROCESS

✓ FREEZE FOR 20 MINUTES

✓ MEANWHILE PREPARE DECORATING SUPPLIES

✓ MELT THE REMAINING CHOCOLATE IN A BOWL. MAKE SURE YOU HAVE ENOUGH
TO SUBMERGE THE ENTIRE CAKE BALL.

✓ REMOVE CAKE BALLS FROM FREEZER

✓ DIP CAKE BALLS CAREFULLY INTO THE CHOCOLATE UNTIL COVERED.

✓ LET THE EXCESS CHOCOLATE DRIP OFF. SHAKE OR SWIRL IF NECESSARY

✓ ADD THE SPRINKLES WHILE THE CHOCOLATE IS STILL WET.

BAKER'S NOTES

Graduation ceremony day: May 2018! Officially six years of being a Husky and now one with two degrees: BS, MPH!

This is one of my favorite pictures of my dad and I at my MPH graduation! It was just three years prior we were standing on this same quad taking photos after my undergraduate ceremony.

Although I walked across the graduation stage in May, I did not officially hand in and defend my Master's capstone project until August 2018. I remember this moment. I could not believe I was done with school forever, not only done, but I was officially a "Master" of Public Health. I also think this could be on the Northeastern website...just saying!

GET CREATIVE WITH THE DECORATIONS, EXPERIMENT WITH DIFFERENT SPRINKLES AND CANDY FINISHES.

I have been single since the breakup with A, which has brought a lot of unnecessary shame. I write about it here in hopes to debunk the idea that you need a partner to be successful. Don't get me wrong, there is a reason why the idea exists, and the feelings are real. I mean, would *The Bachelor* franchise survive if we all felt comfortable being alone? (Sorry Brenna, I know how much you love *The Bachelor*!) Coming from a Jewish family, with a "yenta" for a mother, I often feel the stereotypical push to find a boyfriend or husband, and while I would love a partner, I am actually really okay doing me right now.

It has taken me a long time to get to this place, and it does not mean I don't renew my JDate subscription from time to time, but as my dad says, it is better to be single than with the wrong person. I definitely worry that the right person will never come. I am an undeniable "E" (in the Myers-Briggs extrovert context), and being with others feels much better than being alone, especially in tough times. I remember how much I yearned for a partner after innocently falling down a flight of stairs and breaking my tailbone in January 2019. The recovery from a broken tailbone was hard to do single. But I figured it out. I relied on my friends and my physical therapist. I got very comfortable using Peapod and DoorDash and picked myself up from quite literally falling on my ass... and I did it single.

It doesn't help though that most of my friends are either in serious relationships or married, but I try not to look at it as a race. I have one mentor, Stephanie Walton, author of *Succeeding with Passion,* who tells her community to stay in the eighth lane. In the eighth lane on a track, you can't see who is in front or behind you. The only way to succeed is to "run your own best race"—something that is incredibly valuable and yet incredibly difficult to remember at the same time.

As hard as it can be to sit with being single at times, I never seem to run out of ideas for experimenting creatively. Sometimes this can make it difficult for me to stick to one idea, and I have so many projects going at once. There is a part of me that truly loves

171

this though; it is how I cope and make sense of things, which is why Dena no longer asks me to take a break from projects. In fact, she doesn't call them projects anymore; she believes it is a brand. Dena has cheered me on in every aspect of this creative career, and in many ways, she has helped model the strength and belief in myself that I want to help others find. While Dena calls this my brand, I am not totally sure what to call it. To me it doesn't feel finished; it may never feel finished, but it is the lens through which I live my life.

—-

It took me about two years to complete my biggest accomplishment thus far: *Bake it Till You Make it: Breaking Bread, Building Resilience.* This mental health and resilience cookbook evolved so much from the time I created the idea to the moment I typed my name in the search bar on Amazon and saw the cover photo pop up. I learned to trust myself and I learned that if someone told me "no, it will never happen" that there is always a way to go around and through. I think the biggest and most beautiful lesson I learned from this process though is what resilience has meant and means to others. This book is a compilation of both recipes and stories: stories representing all different human experiences. From loss to trauma, and anxiety and grief, the book has also given me my largest and tallest platform to stand on. I had a mini book tour, including a birthday book signing, and I began to take my speaking more seriously. Most notably, I have gone back to both PC and NU to tell my story.

This cookbook has continued to change my life in so many ways and has conjured up so much conversation and so much art. From "How Will You Tell Your Story?" workshops to *Bake it Till You Make it: Live*—a part cooking demonstration, part inspirational story—each layer brings more joy. One of the most special experiences so far was the creation and execution of *From The Kitchen.* NU Acting Out, a theater advocacy organization at NU, adapted five of the stories from the book into a play and put it on stage in October 2019. Each experience has continuously inspired me to create: new presentations, new ways to facilitate conversation and new ways to continue to build on these ideas and help the community.

This would not be an authentic account of my life though if I stopped here: As easy as it is to list my accomplishments, taking myself seriously is still hard. Like the way I used grades to measure my "worth" in school, during the process of creating the cookbook, I assigned arbitrary benchmarks to times I could take myself seriously. Like the first time I saw my book on a Barnes & Noble shelf or the first time I would speak at a college, but I quickly realized these benchmarks came and went and I still felt the same. So, I see taking myself seriously as a daily practice. I talk and text about brand ideas with Dena and Kathy. I make calls like I deserve to make them, and I stop at nothing to somehow share my mission. I have had to become creative in teaching and showing myself that I will never find my worth in an arbitrary measure, but it takes time to deconstruct this type of mindset. So, I am instead adopting being gentle with myself and recognize that my best has been, is and always will be enough.

- ✓ PREHEAT THE OVEN TO 350F

- ✓ BEGIN TO MAKE CAKE BY ADDING:
  1 CUP WATER
  1/3 CUP OIL
  3 EGGS

- ✓ MIX INGREDIENTS IN A BOWL

- ✓ BAKE FOR 18-20 MINUTES

- ✓ LET CAKE COOL.

- ✓ ONCE CAKE IS COOLED, CRUMBLE CAKE UNTIL IT RESEMBLES FINE CRUMBS

- ✓ ADD IN TWO CANS OF FROSTING TO THE BOWL OF FINE CRUMBS. ADD IN FROSTING A LITTLE BIT AT A TIME TO ENSURE YOU STILL HAVE A LITTLE CRUMBLE.

- ✓ USING AN ICE CREAM SCOOP OR SPOON, SCOOP TWO CAKE MIXTURE BALLS WORTH OF DOUGH AND ROLL IN A TIGHT BALL.

- ✓ CONTINUE UNTIL ALL DOUGH IS ROLLED INTO TIGHT BALLS

- ✓ MELT TWO TO THREE OUNCES OF YOUR FAVORITE CHOCOLATE IN THE MICROWAVE.

- ✓ DIP THE TIP OF THE CAKE POP STICKS INTO THE CHOCOLATE AND INSERT THEM INTO THE CAKE BALLS ABOUT HALFWAY. THIS WILL SECURE THEM THROUGH THE PROCESS

- ✓ FREEZE FOR 20 MINUTES

- ✓ MEANWHILE PREPARE DECORATING SUPPLIES

- ✓ MELT THE REMAINING CHOCOLATE IN A BOWL. MAKE SURE YOU HAVE ENOUGH TO SUBMERGE THE ENTIRE CAKE BALL.

- ✓ REMOVE CAKE BALLS FROM FREEZER

- ✓ DIP CAKE BALLS CAREFULLY INTO THE CHOCOLATE UNTIL COVERED.

- ✓ LET THE EXCESS CHOCOLATE DRIP OFF. SHAKE OR SWIRL IF NECESSARY

- ✓ ADD THE SPRINKLES WHILE THE CHOCOLATE IS STILL WET.

- ✓ GET CREATIVE WITH THE DECORATIONS, EXPERIMENT WITH DIFFERENT SPRINKLES AND CANDY FINISHES.

BAKER'S NOTES

I could not have survived my tailbone break without this amazing friend, Sarah. She helped me heal both physically and mentally and has become one of my best friends. When I was finally ready to get back to SoulCycle after my injury, I couldn't think of a better person to join me.

This was the moment I found out I would be cele-
brating my birthday at Barnes & Noble after landing
my first book signing at this location! This is the
Barnes & Noble that I grew up going to as a kid
making this birthday evening more meaningful.

Hannah, me, and Mallory at my Barnes & Noble Birthday Book Signing. I was so happy they were there to
celebrate! Mallory is one of my biggest mental health
entrepreneur inspirations as she speaks so eloquently
about her story and has her own self-care box company called Find Your/Self boxes. And Hannah rocks too!!

I wouldn't want to do any of this without Brenna, one of the truest friends I have ever known and the amazing photographer who took all of the photos for *Bake it Till You Make it.*

Categories › Personal Development › Resilience

33 Best New Resilience Books To Read In 2019

As featured on CNN, Forbes and Inc – BookAuthority identifies and rates the best books in the world. Learn more

Recommendations by Angelica Malin, Ava Duvernay, Arianna Huffington, Jenny Mccwahlberg and 11 others

One of the coolest and most random parts of being an author for me is googling myself and finding out my book is making the difference I had always hoped! *Bake it Till You Make it* is number 18 on this list put out by BooksAuthority!

This is a photo of the cast and crew including all of the incredible people who made *From the Kitchen* happen! As someone who grew up on stage seeing something I created come to life in theater was magic!

SoulCycle continued to be a place of refuge for me at this
time in large part because of this instructor, Charlotte!

When I first had the conversation with the production team for *From the Kitchen,* I knew exactly who I wanted to play younger me in the show, my friend, Lilly. Lilly is the daughter of my dear friend, Katherine. Lilly and I have grown close over the years I have known her and she inspires me to live freely and as me! I am happy we got to experience this together and wear matching velvet dresses with combat boots.

This is a photo from my first *Bake it TIll You Make it: Live!* presentation. I told my story while making two different desserts from my book, creating metaphors when speaking about certain ingredients. I did this at NU's Xhibition Kitchen, a test kitchen where celebrity (yes celebrity) chefs come and host demos! I am probably the most inexperienced cook to ever host a presentation at Xhibition Kitchen and yet, I own it, it was awesome and I learned so much!

Hi Dayna! I just wanted to reach out to thank you for your talk at Northeastern! After hearing your story and really connecting with how you were feeling I actually had the courage and direction to go to for an inpatient mental health treatment and really try to get better..so thank you for your bravery of sharing your experiences for others to connect..you helped me without even knowing it!

The best thing that came out of my first *Bake it Till You Make it: Live!* presentation was this message. I live and share with the hope that I will inspire others, knowing that I helped this person seek treatment is everything.

As much as I treasure every time I get the opportunity to speak at my high school, putting my book on the shelf in the library was beyond surreal.

You were wonderful today- thank you for letting me sit in on your presentation. Everything you speak about is what we try to emphasize with our Health classes- empathy and understanding with mental health, self advocacy and self care just to name a few. Your strength and wisdom turly shine through in your words. We are delighted you can come back

This was an email I look back at often! I got this from the Health Teacher at my high school after my presentation and putting my book on the shelf!

This is Jackie, the Community Residence Counselor who changed my life at East House! Learning from and being cared about by Jackie, inspired me to change career paths and tap into the power of my own story from the very beginning. Eight years later I had a book signing at McLean Hospital through "The Cole Resource Center" and Jackie came!

In addition to speaking at colleges and high schools, after releasing my book I got the opportunity to speak at a Senior Center! This was thanks to my friend, April (next to me on the left)! She is one of my biggest supports and a wonderful friend. I loved speaking to the seniors as it is never too late to invest in one's mental health! From left to right: Donna (April's mom), April, me and Andrea.

Speaking at Providence College in February 2020 was surreal to say the least. It was one of the first times I had been back on campus since I left. I am still searching for words to express how this felt.

PLACE CAKE POPS IN A STAND AND SHARE THEM WITH SOMEONE YOU LOVE.

Just like a completed cake pop, I am currently standing in place. There are some predicted certainties (although my dad likes to remind me that the only thing certain in life is that nothing is certain), but I expect to continue working at a youth-serving organization in my community. While my job does not explicitly entail working on mental health initiatives, I love that I have had the opportunity to connect with so many teens over the years who have felt comfortable sharing their own stories with me. If I have learned anything from connecting with so many youth over the years, it is that they are the role models. They are resilient and creative in all ways, and I plan on continuing to be inspired by them both today and forever. (As corny as that sounds, it's the truth.)

I also plan on continuing to stand confidently as a role model for my youngest and coolest friend, Lilly, the ten-year-old daughter of my dear friend Katherine. Lilly told me as soon as I met her she is "the bold type." She is not afraid to be herself, and I love her for it. I plan to stand tall for her, to be honest about my struggles and let her know that it is okay not to be okay.

I stand for all of my friends, those in my life who are inspirations to me, especially those like Yas, who are continuously knocked down but choose to get back up.

I plan on standing even in the moments I do not feel okay, because I know I have a team behind me, but honestly, if I didn't, I think I would make it work. Dena used to tell me to practice the mantra "come hell or high water, I will be okay" I couldn't ever imagine feeling connected with this statement, but I am proud to say, as I am writing this, in a lot of ways I do.

I still worry about my mom and my family, I still worry about vomit, but there are some moments I feel I truly worry about everything. I have tried, though, to lead with love. I see that I worry because I love, and I love big. Even though I used to think it was "too much," I see it is just right for me.

—-

If there is anything I have learned at twenty-seven years old it is that even when I stand in place, I am always looking to share. Kathy has always said that even when there is a setback, you never start back at the original square one, and I love that because I feel I share at every square.

There is a reason the titles of both of my books are actionable, because I stand for action. I stand for taking things that people don't talk about, writing about them, yelling about them and making them okay. I stand and share because I do not want anyone to have to experience what I did. I stand because I feel I have a responsibility to create, change and advocate. I stand because I always have and I always will.

—-

If I could tell anything to that scared little girl that still lives inside of me, it is that there is love for you. You may not feel it, you may not get it in the way that you want, but it doesn't mean that you are unlovable. You are worthy of the love you put out, and for some that means you are the brightest light they may see. I hope you begin to see your own light, Dayna, the one that has always been there to guide you home, back into the home you have created, the one inside.

✓ PREHEAT THE OVEN TO 350F

✓ BEGIN TO MAKE CAKE BY ADDING:
1 CUP WATER
1/3 CUP OIL
3 EGGS

✓ MIX INGREDIENTS IN A BOWL

✓ BAKE FOR 18-20 MINUTES

✓ LET CAKE COOL.

✓ ONCE CAKE IS COOLED, CRUMBLE CAKE UNTIL IT RESEMBLES FINE CRUMBS

✓ ADD IN TWO CANS OF FROSTING TO THE BOWL OF FINE CRUMBS. ADD IN
FROSTING A LITTLE BIT AT A TIME TO ENSURE YOU STILL HAVE A LITTLE
CRUMBLE.

✓ USING AN ICE CREAM SCOOP OR SPOON, SCOOP TWO CAKE MIXTURE BALLS
WORTH OF DOUGH AND ROLL IN A TIGHT BALL.

✓ CONTINUE UNTIL ALL DOUGH IS ROLLED INTO TIGHT BALLS

✓ MELT TWO TO THREE OUNCES OF YOUR FAVORITE CHOCOLATE IN THE
MICROWAVE.

✓ DIP THE TIP OF THE CAKE POP STICKS INTO THE CHOCOLATE AND INSERT
THEM INTO THE CAKE BALLS ABOUT HALFWAY. THIS WILL SECURE THEM
THROUGH THE PROCESS

✓ FREEZE FOR 20 MINUTES

✓ MEANWHILE PREPARE DECORATING SUPPLIES

✓ MELT THE REMAINING CHOCOLATE IN A BOWL. MAKE SURE YOU HAVE ENOUGH
TO SUBMERGE THE ENTIRE CAKE BALL.

✓ REMOVE CAKE BALLS FROM FREEZER

✓ DIP CAKE BALLS CAREFULLY INTO THE CHOCOLATE UNTIL COVERED.

✓ LET THE EXCESS CHOCOLATE DRIP OFF. SHAKE OR SWIRL IF NECESSARY

✓ ADD THE SPRINKLES WHILE THE CHOCOLATE IS STILL WET.

✓ GET CREATIVE WITH THE DECORATIONS, EXPERIMENT WITH DIFFERENT
SPRINKLES AND CANDY FINISHES.

✓ PLACE CAKE POPS IN STAND AND SHARE THEM WITH SOMEONE YOU LOVE.

BAKER'S NOTES

I will continue to stand and vow to make a difference in the lives of youth everywhere. This is from
the Annual Young Women's Conference 2019. I
am with Jess, who continues to be a role model
and friend to me as she does the same, 143.

I will always stand for my friend, Lilly, who happens to be so strong, beautiful and a fellow Dunkin' lover.

I will continue to stand for people like my friend, Yas, who is continuously challenged and gets back up every single time, wow.

I stand for friendship! Like my connection with my incredible friend, Laura--who always gives me a lift.

I will continue to stand with other organizations that are
doing such wonderful things to change the world. This
photo is from the Out of the Darkness Walk for Suicide
Prevention at NU in 2017. From left to right: Kyle, Jenna,
Becky and I. We are all wearing shirts that say "AMAZ-
ING" backwards as part of Jenna's non-profit organization "The AMAZING Campaign" where she sells shirts,
among other merchandise with empowering messages
encouraging self love. The original shirt says "AMAZING"
backwards so when you look in the mirror, you can see
(and read) how amazing you are.

As I have continued to be an advocate and a well known story teller, I have had some amazing opportunities to share on large scales, like this one! I told my story for SoulCycle's campaign "Soul People are the Best People" on their international IGTV! It was an incredible day sharing my story with a company that has impacted me in so many ways.

I will always worry about my mom, always AND I
will always love her, always. I will always need her
and I will always be by her side.

Where it all began and where it will always lead. My sister, Jamie, my mom, me and my dad in front of that blue house in Southboro MA.

This is home

Southborough

And it wouldn't be home without Dunkin'!

The person I will always fight for as I choose every day to own my story and find my freedom.

Dayna Altman is a bold and authentic mental health entrepreneur, author and public health professional based in Boston MA. A dual graduate of Northeastern University: MPH '18, BS Human Services '15, Dayna brings both professional experience and personal expertise into the work she does for her community. Dayna has held several roles in the human services field working with youth in mental health settings and women who have experienced domestic or sexual violence. She has also created several of her own advocacy organizations specializing in mental health advocacy. Her entrepreneurial adventures have helped her become a professional speaker, a documentary filmmaker, and an author of two books, using food to create a palatable and accessible way for all to approach mental health.

EPILOGUE

Baking has been the unexpected and unsung hero of the COVID-19 pandemic. In order to manage the increased stress, isolation and boredom of stay-at-home orders and quarantine, we have had to find new activities, hobbies and innovations. Many of us have re-discovered the art of baking.

So why are we baking? We bake because it gives us something to have mastery over, a project we can control from start to finish. We bake because it evokes our senses in wonderful ways, creating aromas, tastes and textures to soothe us. We bake because home-made sourdough and banana breads reminds of a time, perhaps a fictional or fantasy era that we have never even known, in which life was not so challenging and we were not so frightened.

None of this is new to Dayna, she has known for quite some time that baking can be healing and serve as a metaphor for life. We saw this metaphor unfold as Dayna courageously shared her story and journey towards mental health recovery with us. This is not the end of Dayna's story. We can look forward to her continued advocacy on behalf of those who struggle with mental illness and for those who face stigma or shame in accessing mental health care. Dayna will continue to bring us innovative programs, pod-casts and workshops to help us discover our own individual recipe for mental health.

I have known Dayna for many years and I am deeply proud of the work she has done and the person she has become. When I met her, I could see she had all of raw ingredients within herself to work through and manage her pain. It has been a true joy in my life to watch her mix, melt and mend into the brave and wonderful woman she is today. I look forward to what lies ahead.

Dena B Tranen, LCSW

Hi there!

Scan this code to be brought to the official website of Bake it Till You Make it org! Here you can purchase the supplemental *Mix, Melt, Mend* workbook. The workbook has activity pages, journal prompts, extra recipes and instructions on how to create a discussion group or forum to discuss the themes of this book. Groups can be created for corporate wellness programs, those in treatment facilities or among friends. Feel free to email bakeitcookbook@gmail.com for further inquiries about purchasing the workbook in bulk or hiring Dayna to facilitate the group herself.

To get a "taste" of the workbook, check out the next few pages!

Reflection Questions: Part One
Preheat The Oven to 350F

General Reflection: How did you feel reading this section?

2. How did your environment impact your childhood? How about your life as an adult?

3. What were your greatest challenges in childhood? What coping skills did you use?

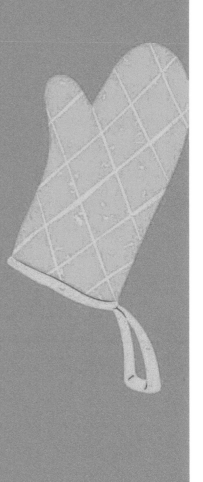

4. Dayna shares with the reader that her external appearance and her internal experience were very different. Does this resonate with you?

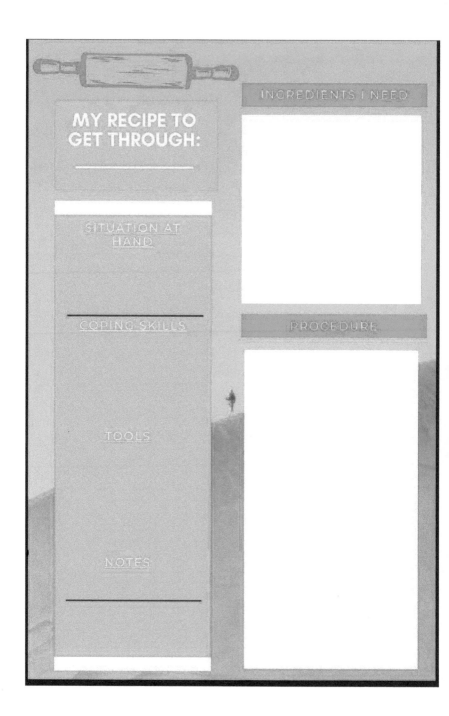

MY RECIPE TO GET THROUGH:

_____

INGREDIENTS I NEED

SITUATION AT HAND

COPING SKILLS

PROCEDURE

TOOLS

NOTES

How to be
"gentle with yourself"

If you have been to therapy before, you may have heard this phrase. Being gentle can be difficult. Here are some suggestions:

"The Friend Test"

Imagine speaking to yourself the way you would speak to a friend. If you wouldn't say it to a friend, it's not ok to say it to yourself.

Prepare for this Moment

If being gentle with yourself is something that you struggle with, try preparing for this moment. Create an affirmation card you can return to, make a list of people you can call or write a letter to your future self.

"Put the Binoculars Down"

It's ok to take a step back. Oftentimes, when we are too close to a situation, it is hard to decide what to do without getting frustrated. Set a timer; take 30 minutes, an hour, a day. It's ok to step back from it, as long as you come back to it and be kind to yourself.

Body Positivity Check with Laura

Body positivity and breaking down the ideal body image has always been a mission that I have held close to my heart, especially as my struggle started in my early years of college. In the past, I have always felt that my experience with body image issues and anxiety were not worth talking about. After I met Dayna, she gave me affirmation that everyone's story is enough. This is so important to remember because I truly believe that telling your story can set you free! Just be you! - Laura McCoy

Self Care Check with Jules

Taking care of your mental health is a huge component of self-care and self-love, and sometimes that means realizing when you need to ask for help. Don't be afraid to do this (easier said than done), and don't feel guilty for asking for what you need. Even if you don't feel comfortable reaching out to a professional just yet, remember that you have a support system already in place — your friends, family members, and other loved ones! - Julia Guilardi